DON'T
Count Me Out

Sermons from the
Bahamian Pulpit

BISHOP WELLINGTON WILLIAMS

WESTBOW
PRESS®
A DIVISION OF THOMAS NELSON
& ZONDERVAN

WestBow Press books may be ordered through booksellers or by contacting:

WestBow Press
A Division of Thomas Nelson & Zondervan
1663 Liberty Drive
Bloomington, IN 47403
www.westbowpress.com
1 (866) 928-1240

Scriptures marked NIV are taken from the NEW INTERNATIONAL VERSION (NIV): Scripture taken from THE HOLY BIBLE, NEW INTERNATIONAL VERSION ®. Copyright© 1973, 1978, 1984, 2011 by Biblica, Inc.™. Used by permission of Zondervan

All other scriptures are taken from the KING JAMES VERSION (KJV): KING JAMES VERSION, public domain.

ISBN: 978-1-9736-8956-0 (sc)
ISBN: 978-1-9736-8958-4 (hc)
ISBN: 978-1-9736-8957-7 (e)

Library of Congress Control Number: 2020910843

Print information available on the last page.

WestBow Press rev. date: 07/21/2020

ACKNOWLEDGMENTS

First, let me thank the almighty God for His unending faithfulness and the supernatural impact He has placed on my life. He is the one who continues to amaze me by downloading revelations, wisdom, and mind-boggling abilities.

Thank you, Shamanique, for your continued prayers and encouragement. May God's richest blessings be upon you.

To my well-wishers both in the Bahamas and abroad, thank you for believing in me and for your continued prayers. I will forever be grateful indeed.

To God be the glory. Great things He has done.

INTRODUCTION

Brothers and sisters, I greet you in the matchless name of our Lord and Savior, Jesus the Christ. As I scroll through the Bible, I am challenged to broaden my understanding and experience a deeper appreciation for the Creator as He unveils His magnificence by preparing the earth to accommodate humankind.

In His mind, I can only imagine how He uniquely and purposely designed a world to sustain whatever and whomever it was created for. History has revealed that there are several planets in the galaxy that can accommodate life. Humankind is desperately seeking ways to transfer or relocate life to those other planets, knowing full well that the earth was created by the Creator Himself for humankind to live on and rule it.

> And God said, Let the waters under the heaven be gathered together unto one place, and let the dry land appear: and it was so. And God called the dry land Earth; and the gathering together of the waters called he Seas: and God saw that it was good. And God said, Let the earth bring forth grass, the herb yielding seed, and the fruit tree yielding fruit after his kind, whose seed

is in itself, upon the earth: and it was so. And the earth brought forth grass, and herb yielding seed after his kind, and the tree yielding fruit, whose seed was in itself, after his kind: and God saw that it was good. (Genesis 1:9–12 KJV)

According to Genesis 2:7, God reveals Himself as all-sufficient, all-knowing, and sovereign. After God created everything, He created humankind from the dust of the earth and breathed the breath of life into Adam's nostril, and he became a living soul. This expresses His love for us and the significance of having the ability to rule "The heaven, even the heavens, are the Lord's: but the earth hath he given to the children of men" (Psalm 115:16 KJV).

One should realize that the preparation for a thing is as equally important as what it's being prepared for.

Now everything has been created, prepared, and provided to humankind. Humanity now has full dominion, but there's still a major void. It is very transparent, but it cannot be recognized by the natural or carnal sight. This is called the absence of the ability to understand.

There are four extremely important dimensions that are not well known but are essential for the smooth correlation between God and people and the existence of humankind on earth. They are as follows:

- Listening: Listening, like the other three dimensions, is not an ability but a gift.
- Observation: This is the ability to confidently scan a thing, an area, or even an individual.

- Processing: This is the ability to assess, cautiously meditate (think) about, or ponder something.
- Decision-making: This is the ability to make unmistakably effective judgments/decisions. Any decision, judgment, or ruling that is made without the engagement of these four rules for success will create the need for regrets, apologies, and/or replacement, because a mistake is present.

I have discovered that for decades, leaders from all walks have tried to mislead those who would lend them an ear for whatever reason, and this includes the church. When people fail to listen, they usually face a number of conundrums. We are mandated by the universal God to obey His commands in their entirety, to study to show ourselves approved unto God (2 Timothy 2:15), and to go into the world and make disciples, teaching and preaching to all nations (Matthew 28:19–20).

The purpose of this book is to help reroute the Word of God to its original position so that its purpose can be reestablished. This publication will address the dire need for people's clarity, restoration, strength, and recovery.

CHAPTER 1

Don't Count Me Out

And Jesus answering said, A certain man went down from Jerusalem to Jericho, and fell among thieves, which stripped him of his raiment, and wounded him, and departed, leaving him half dead. And by chance there came down a certain priest that way: and when he saw him, he passed by on the other side. And likewise a Levite, when he was at the place, came and looked on him, and passed by on the other side. But a certain Samaritan, as he journeyed, came where he was: and when he saw him, he had compassion on him, And went to him, and bound up his wounds, pouring in oil and wine, and set him on his own beast, and brought him to an inn, and took care of him. And on the morrow when he departed, he took out two pence, and gave them to the host, and said unto him, Take care of him; and whatsoever thou spendest more, when I come again, I will repay thee. Which now of these three, thinkest thou, was neighbour unto him that fell among the thieves? And he said, He that shewed mercy on him. Then said Jesus unto him, Go, and do thou likewise. (Luke 10:30–37 KJV)

Many human beings are affected by major issues that are distressing. These issues may include domestic, church-related, or national issues—the list goes on. Some are sincerely confused about these issues. Some folks just cannot get along with anyone. They do not have the ability to coexist or see the necessity to coexist with others. But we as believers have been instructed to do so.

The Bible says in Romans 12:18 that if it is possible, as far as it depends on you, live peaceably with all people.

It suggests that God is aware that these issues exist. When we give everything over to God, He promises that He will never leave nor forsake us. He also promises that He will be our way of escape. It now becomes a matter of trusting His Word.

I could not tell which of these issues the young man in Luke 10:30–37 was caught up in, but what I can say is that he fell among thieves and was stripped of his clothing, beaten, wounded, and left half-dead.

We know that the cultures of Jews and the Samaritan were distinctly different. This kept them pretty much separated from each other.

Ezekiel 16:47–48 suggests that Samaria was a corrupt and wicked city. Many countries, including the Bahamas, seem to be an extension of the Samaritan culture.

You not only followed their ways and copied their detestable practices, but in all your ways you soon became more depraved than they. As surely as I live, declares the Sovereign Lord, your sister Sodom and her daughters never did what you and your daughters have done. (Ezekiel 16:47–48 NIV)

According to 2 Kings 17:29, Samaria was a city that built and worshipped idols. This segregation occurred up to the reign of Christ. As a result, Samaria was considered a rejected city. For this reason, the Jews had no dealings with the Samaritans. This was one of the reasons why Jesus found it necessary to go to Samaria. "And he must needs go through Samaria" (John 4:4 KJV).

The road to Jericho from Jerusalem was steep, rocky, winding one and was notorious for its dangers and difficulties. It was known as the way of blood because of the blood that was often shed there by robbers. Jericho is located north of the Dead Sea. It is about fifteen miles east of Jerusalem. I will compare this road to Bass Lane, Kemp Road, East Street, or Bain Town. These are streets found in Grand Bahama and Nassau respectively. These areas are known for various crimes, such as armed robbery, looting, rape, and murder. These areas have the potential for constant, imminent danger. If you get out, thank God, and if you do not get out unscathed, you expect it because this is what happens.

Something was bound to happen if you walked in those areas, whether you were protected or alone, whether it was day or night. I suspect the young man in the parable was a Jew. And so, being ambushed by gangsters, he found himself in problems. He was found half-dead. But to the amazement of passersby, he was half-alive also.

You may be experiencing difficulties. You may be in a similar situation where you are physically or emotionally battered, feeling half-dead. You may have been rejected, insulted, or neglected—either by friends or by church folks, as is often the case for whatever reason.

> Thou therefore endure hardness, as a good soldier of Jesus Christ. No man that warreth entangleth himself with the affairs of this life; that he may please him who hath chosen him to be a soldier. And if a man also strive for masteries, yet is he not crowned, except he strive lawfully. (2 Timothy 2:3–5 KJV)

Don't feel because you are going through difficult times that you are alone. God has promised that no matter where you are, He is there. "If I ascend up into heaven, thou art there: if I make my bed in hell, behold thou art there" (Psalm 139:8 KJV).

He will never leave you nor forsake you, which is reiterated in other scriptures:

> Be strong and of a good courage, fear not, nor be afraid of them: for the Lord thy God, he it is that doth go with thee; he will not fail thee, nor forsake thee. (Deuteronomy 31:6 KJV)

Let your conversation be without covetousness; and be content with such things as ye have: for he hath said, I will never leave thee, nor forsake thee. So that we may boldly say, The Lord is my helper, and I will not fear what man shall do unto me. (Hebrews 13:5–6 KJV)

The young man in the parable was down but not out, battered but not denied. You are not *going* through; you should be *growing* through. Do not focus on what you are going through. Concentrate on where you are going to, as evidenced by the following scriptures:

But you, keep your head in all situations, endure hardship, do the work of an evangelist, discharge all the duties of your ministry. (2 Timothy 4:5 NIV)

Not only so, but we also glory in our sufferings, because we know that suffering produces perseverance; perseverance, character; and character, hope. And hope does not put us to shame, because God's love has been poured out into our hearts through the Holy Spirit, who has been given to us. (Romans 5:3–5 NIV)

Perhaps the young man thought to himself, *I might be half-dead, but I'm half-alive. I am still vested with abilities, so don't count me out. All my faculties are intact, just a little immobilized.*

This battered young man felt hopeless; he was on the brink of throwing in the towel. Can you imagine being in a condition like that? You might even be in or have experienced a situation like that. Being in the wrong place at the wrong time can cause the wrong thing to happen.

The wrong thing happened to you in the wrong area of life. You may be in the midst of the wrong outcome. You may be overwhelmed with a catastrophic outcome. There is no one to help. The odds are against you; you are wounded and naked. It's beginning to get dark. You're losing blood. This couldn't get worse.

You are not at home and not where you are supposed to be. The young man thought to himself, *I may as well give up. I don't know of many who have traveled this road who fell under these circumstances and survived.*

In those days, culture was a serious thing. It meant that what the people who lived in that area were dealing with was what they clung to. According to the Bible, the priest saw the young man and passed on the other side. Likewise, the Levite only looked on and passed by. Bit by bit, the young man's chances for rescue were getting slimmer. *What's next?* he thought.

Nothing has changed today. Some folks use the office of pastor, priest, or evangelist for personal gratification, while the sheep are being spiritually traumatized, ambushed, and scattered—only to find out that they are being misled by hirelings. This priest who passed by demonstrates this well. The Bible says in Jeremiah 23:1–3 (KJV),

> "Woe be unto the pastors that destroy and scatter the sheep of my pasture!" saith the Lord. Therefore thus saith the Lord God of Israel

against the pastors that feed my people; Ye have scattered my flock, and driven them away, and have not visited them: behold, I will visit upon you the evil of your doings, saith the Lord. And I will gather the remnant of my flock out of all countries whither I have driven them, and will bring them again to their folds; and they shall be fruitful and increase.

So we find that in all cases when you feel that you are down to nothing, God is definitely up to something. I want to say to you that if God is for you, no one can be against you. Thank God for His grace and mercy, for had it not been for grace and mercy, the young man would have died.

He was left lying on the ground, and he began to bleed profusely. If you understand how the human body functions, you will know that your life is your blood. You can survive the loss of many body parts, but when you start to lose a lot of blood, that's another matter. You're just about done.

As the young man began to lose blood, he began to lose strength.

As he began to lose strength, he began to lose vision.

As he began to lose vision, he began to lose focus.

As he began to lose focus, he began to lose fight.

As he began to lose fight, his hope was fading into the sunset.

Once this began to happen, he looked forward to an unexpected end. But the Good Samaritan showed up and hope began to come alive.

When you look at this story, you'll find that the people of

God are slackening their ride and are not interested in their duties. But the Samaritan, who was known not to deal with people of the Jewish nationality, was on a journey. He was on duty when he stopped and came to where the man was struggling for his life. When he saw his condition, he had compassion on him. This is the very thing a church should do. It should not ignore or overlook a person in the midst of a spiritual battle.

I was once told the only time you look down on a person is when you are picking him or her up.

Romans 5:8 (KJV) says, "We all have sinned and come short of the Glory of God." If we ignore a spiritually battered person, we become equivalent to him or her. Our actions will condemn us.

The Good Samaritan not only had compassion, but he also attended to the man's injuries by pouring oil and wine on them. He set him on his beast and took him to an inn for further care. He left an open check in case the man needed anything extra. When he passed back, he would pick up the tab.

Today I'm living proof that the price for our sin is paid in full. According to 1 John 2:1, Jesus paid the price for you and me in full.

Some folks believe that the priest and the Levite may have been afraid to stop because it was known that this road was very dangerous and, taking the time into consideration, thought it was not wise to stop. They failed to realize that God did not give them the spirit of fear but of love and of a sound mind. This is where personal agenda comes in. They allowed their personal agendas to interfere with their Christian duty.

Not many are concerned about obedience. But obedience is better than sacrifice according to 1 Samuel 15:22. As Christians, you will be faced with many trials. But you should not allow fear, prejudice, or lack of knowledge to paralyze you in the execution of duty.

When the Levite and the priest passed the injured traveler by, that action suggests that they were about their own business.

Today it does not matter where you are, what you encounter, how it may appear, or if you only let the mind that was in Christ Jesus be also in you. There will be no room for personal agenda. What you think and how you feel have nothing to do with it. It is all about the Father's business, no more, no less. Once you're dealing with your personal agenda, chances are you have already abandoned your duty. Then your purpose for living has been reduced to a sounding brass and a tinkling symbol—only talk and nothing to show for it. This seems to be the standard almost everywhere you go.

Today this parable places you and me in this man's position. How often are we left bruised, battered, horrified, and rejected by our very own? How often do we feel talked about and criticized by people we least expect it from? This may include your coworkers, family, friends, or even members of your church family.

This causes spirits of hatred, bitterness, jealousy, and envy to rise up among the believers. Before you know it, it's over. Those who look up to us are becoming stagnant. If this is how the pacesetters are leading, what are we supposed to do?

And for this among other reasons, the Bible says if the righteous are scarcely saved, where shall the sinners and ungodly appear? Woe to the shepherd and pastors who scatter His sheep.

The road ahead is colorful. Difficulties, hopelessness, and hardship are among the inevitable. But the Lord will deliver you out of them all. People you expect to behave a certain way are going to do the contrary. These people are the very ones who backstab and cut down everything good. They are the root cause of the church being sabotaged and undermined.

This why God says in 1 Peter 4:17 (KJV), "For the time is come that judgment must begin at the house of God: and if it first begin at us, what shall the end be of them that obey not the gospel of God?"

These are the people you think would have your back. But I am reminded of the scripture Micah 7: 5 (KJV), which says, "Trust ye not in a friend, put ye not confidence in a guide: keep the doors of thy mouth from her that lieth in thy bosom."

But I thank God for Jesus, the ultimate Good Samaritan. He's the Samaritan who did not reject me. The one who did not pass by on the other side. The one who picked me up, cleansed my wounds, took me to the inn, and paid the price. The one who has left an open account at the inn. The one who told me the bill was paid in full.

He told me, "I've got your back." Then he turns around and says, "I will never leave you nor forsake you. I'll be with you until the end." To Him be all the glory, honor, and praise

Today, His name is Jesus.

Come now, and let us reason together, saith the Lord: though your sins be as scarlet, they shall be as white as snow; though they be red like crimson, they shall be as wool. If ye be willing and obedient, ye shall eat the good of the land. (Isaiah 1:18–19 KJV)

He is still saying, "Come unto me all ye that are labored and are heavy laden and I will give you rest" (Matthew 11:28 KJV). Rest from your physical labor, rest from your mental enslavement, rest from your sacrifices, rest from the spiritual hemorrhages that the world is sadly faced with. Whether black, white, rich, or poor, it does not matter your condition, come and buy oil and wine without money and without pride.

Praise the name of the Lord, the Most High.

The battered man thought to himself, *Throughout all those episodes, I was half-dead but half-alive, so don't count me out. I am physically devastated. I do not know what's going on, but don't count me out. I am lying down all busted up by thieves and stripped of my raiment, but don't count me out.*

I have been lied about. I have been set up by peers so they can look better in the eyes of people. I have been on the wait list forever, but don't count me out.

The Good Samaritan is here. I will get oil and wine I don't have to pay for. I will survive this one. I am half-dead, but I will have you to know I am half-alive, so don't count me out.

Even though the medication was not yet administered, hope began to come alive due to the presence of the Good Samaritan. The young man felt protected and loved. He recognized healing and full recovery. The light of despair was in the process of disappearing. A spring and a rising of a new day were beginning to appear.

This one is on God. I can tell you like He told Hezekiah, it isn't unto death. Through it all, I've learned to trust in Jesus. But if I never had a problem, I would never have known that God could solve it, and all my trials just came to make me strong. Today I'm pleased to report to you that my life is still in me. So don't count me out. I am a work in progress, thanks be to God.

I thank God today that I am alive and doing well. Someone saw me when I was sinking. Somebody rescued me from among the thieves. Someone dusted me off and saw value in me. Jesus gave me a new lease on life, and He is seated at the right hand of the Father interceding for you and for me. I know what it means to be left hopeless. I know how it feels to be set free.

I can recall sometime during the mid-1990s my integrity was called into question regarding a major crime I was alleged to have been a part of. One night, I was invited to a christening party by a friend who was also a colleague. Once I got there, he introduced me to two other colleagues and told me they were his friends. When the function ended, I did not have a ride home, so he asked them to give me a ride home. We all got in the vehicle. They drove me home. Once I got home, my friend told me he would call me in a few hours.

I was expecting to hear from him as he was a man of his word. When I did not hear from him, I started to become concerned. I called him. But the phone only went to voice mail each time. I suspected something had happened. I went to inquire about his whereabouts. I was met by another colleague who asked me if I had heard about a suspected murder. Murder? He went on to fill me in on the details. He said the body of a male had been found in the western area of New Providence, Arawak Cay, with gunshot wounds to the back. On hearing that, I immediately went to my car, and we drove to Arawak. I saw investigators and familiar faces. As I got out the car and got closer to the scene, I recognized my friend. He was lying facedown on the ground. I walked over and identified him. I told the officers that I had seen him a few hours ago because he had dropped me at home a few hours earlier. As a result, I was considered a suspect and invited to the criminal investigation department, escorted by a team of investigating officers.

To my surprise, I was a murder suspect! I had no knowledge other than knowing the deceased and the perpetrators he introduced me to (his killers). Being taken into custody, I thought to myself, *If you did nothing, you should fear nothing.* To my surprise, I was arrested as a murder suspect. I did not realize the seriousness of the matter until I saw for the second time the two other suspects. Then I remembered them as the people the deceased introduced me to, only to find out they were responsible for the actual killing, whether it was accidental or not. As the day went by, I began to pray. Things began to get gloomy. As I began to pray, all my hopes began to fade away. I began reasoning with God once I heard the gentlemen debating legal representation. I said. "Lord, you know I am not guilty of anything." Many scriptures began flowing through my thoughts. The one that stuck with me was Isaiah 41:10 (KJV):

Fear thou not; for I am with thee: be not dismayed; for I am thy God: I will strengthen thee; yea, I will help thee; yea, I will uphold thee with the right hand of my righteousness.

Based on this scripture, I knew that God would be with me until the end. Suddenly, there was a peace. Then I heard one of the young men say to the other, "He really does not know anything about this. This is between you and me." The young man immediately called the supervisor for the shift at the criminal investigation department. He began to relay the events that led to death of our colleague. The supervisor asked me to write a report and told me I was free to go.

I am a living testimony today. Look at the bruises, and check my record. I was there. I didn't have any money, I didn't have any clothes on, but I was clothed in His righteousness and still standing tall. I am dressed in the whole armor of God. I am running the race that has been set before me. I am looking unto Jesus, who is the author and the finisher of my faith. You would imagine I was dead. But wounded isn't dead, and down doesn't mean out. So don't count me out.

Jesus's wounded hand touched my mind. While I was recovering, He put a new praise in my mouth. He put worship in my spirit. He put a dance in my feet and clapping in my hands. So today, I do not have to give you a testimony. I am a testimony.

I can tell the world today, even if this Jew was dead, the Good Samaritan was qualified to say, "Come forth." He is an on-time God. Yes, He is! When nothing else could have helped, His love lifted me. It doesn't matter what your condition is today. Look at what the Lord has done, and just as He has delivered me, He's able to deliver you. Wherever you go, tell the world, "Don't count me out."

CHAPTER 2

I've Got to Close the Door

2 Kings 4:8–37

And it fell on a day, that Elisha passed to Shunem, where was a great woman; and she constrained him to eat bread. And so it was, that as oft as he passed by, he turned in thither to eat bread.

And she said unto her husband, Behold now, I perceive that this is an holy man of God, which passeth by us continually.

Let us make a little chamber, I pray thee, on the wall; and let us set for him there a bed, and a table, and a stool, and a candlestick: and it shall be, when he cometh to us, that he shall turn in thither.

And it fell on a day, that he came thither, and he turned into the chamber, and lay there.

And he said to Gehazi his servant, Call this Shunammite. And when he had called her, she stood before him.

17

And he said unto him, Say now unto her, Behold, thou hast been careful for us with all this care; what is to be done for thee? wouldest thou be spoken for to the king, or to the captain of the host? And she answered, I dwell among mine own people.

And he said, What then is to be done for her? And Gehazi answered, Verily she hath no child, and her husband is old.

And he said, Call her. And when he had called her, she stood in the door.

And he said, About this season, according to the time of life, thou shalt embrace a son. And she said, Nay, my lord, thou man of God, do not lie unto thine handmaid.

And the woman conceived, and bare a son at that season that Elisha had said unto her, according to the time of life.

And when the child was grown, it fell on a day, that he went out to his father to the reapers.

And he said unto his father, My head, my head. And he said to a lad, Carry him to his mother.

And when he had taken him, and brought him to his mother, he sat on her knees till noon, and then died.

And she went up, and laid him on the bed of the man of God, and shut the door upon him, and went out.

And she called unto her husband, and said, Send me, I pray thee, one of the young men, and one of the asses, that I may run to the man of God, and come again.

And he said, Wherefore wilt thou go to him to day? it is neither new moon, nor sabbath. And she said, It shall be well.

Then she saddled an ass, and said to her servant, Drive, and go forward; slack not thy riding for me, except I bid thee.

So she went and came unto the man of God to mount Carmel. And it came to pass, when the man of God saw her afar off, that he said to Gehazi his servant, Behold, yonder is that Shunammite:

Run now, I pray thee, to meet her, and say unto her, Is it well with thee? is it well with thy husband? is it well with the child? And she answered, It is well:

And when she came to the man of God to the hill, she caught him by the feet: but Gehazi came near to thrust her away. And the man of God said, Let her alone; for her soul is vexed within her: and the Lord hath hid it from me, and hath not told me.

Then she said, Did I desire a son of my lord? did I not say, Do not deceive me?

Then he said to Gehazi, Gird up thy loins, and take my staff in thine hand, and go thy way: if thou meet any man, salute him not; and if any salute thee, answer him not again: and lay my staff upon the face of the child.

And the mother of the child said, As the Lord liveth, and as thy soul liveth, I will not leave thee. And he arose, and followed her.

And Gehazi passed on before them, and laid the staff upon the face of the child; but there was neither voice, nor hearing. Wherefore he went again to meet him, and told him, saying, The child is not awaked.

And when Elisha was come into the house, behold, the child was dead, and laid upon his bed.

He went in therefore, and shut the door upon them twain, and prayed unto the Lord.

And he went up, and lay upon the child, and put his mouth upon his mouth, and his eyes upon his eyes, and his hands upon his hands: and stretched himself upon the child; and the flesh of the child waxed warm.

Then he returned, and walked in the house to and fro; and went up, and stretched himself upon him: and the child sneezed seven times, and the child opened his eyes.

And he called Gehazi, and said, Call this Shunammite. So he called her. And when she was come in unto him, he said, Take up thy son.

Then she went in, and fell at his feet, and bowed herself to the ground, and took up her son, and went out.

As the story is told, the prophet Elisha had a servant whose name was Gehazi, and they frequented the city of Shunem. It came a time that a Shunamite woman showed hospitality to these men. On one of the occasions, while the Man of God was there, he said to his servant Gehazi to call the Shunamite and find out how he could be of assistance to her because of the kindness shown to them. The servant told the Man of God that she had no children and that her husband was old. On learning this, the Man of God called for this Shunamite and prophesied to her telling her that at about the same time the following year, she would embrace a son. She refused to acknowledge the prophecy. The day came when the woman conceived and had a son, in accordance to the prophecy. The time came when this young man went into the field with his father and while in the field, he begun to experience a severe headache, so his father sent him to his mother who took him and at noon he died on her lap. So she took the lad and laid him on the bed of the man of God and closed the door. Being troubled in her heart, she told her husband to send one of the young men and one of the donkeys, that she may go to the Man of God and come again. Her husband somehow became concerned and asked, "why are you going to the man of God, what had happened?" she responded, "It shall be well" She saddled the donkey and instructed the servants to drive, and not to slack his ride unless she say otherwise. In other words, she did not have time to waste. As she approached Mt. Carmel, the Man of God saw her afar and sent his servant to meet her. The child's condition was revealed to the prophet. After a brief deliberation with Elisha, he sent the servant to the house where the child was to lay his staff on the child's face, and nothing happened. But when Elisha proceeded to the upper room where the child lay and closed the door, the situation took a turn for the better.

There are times in life when you will be faced with trials that will demand that doors be closed. Many times, tragedy occurs. Before you know it, the important working spaces are filled with onlookers and bystanders, and certain evidence is either destroyed, contaminated, or removed. In a case like this, I don't think anyone needs any of the above.

Working as a law enforcement officer, I have had the chance to experience the importance of cutting off or running the tape between a crime scene and pedestrians. If it's not there, the scene can be compromised. In cases where a crime is committed indoors, the area is cordoned off and the doors are shut while the investigation continues inside.

But in this case, it was a situation between Elisha and God. This was not for the woman or for a middleman. This was something that had to happen. In Bahamian terms, it was a "gotta happen." The past and the future merged to establish the now, to bring about a manifestation of a miraculous urgency. The child was dead. Elisha began to pray and petition

God. He began to cry to the living God. He was comforted by Psalm 91:15–16 (KJV): "He shall call upon me and I will answer him: I will be with him in trouble; I will deliver him, and honor him. With long life I will satisfy him, and shew him my salvation."

The Bible says in Psalm 46:1 (KJV), "God is our refuge and strength, a very present help in time of trouble." He had to be called upon. He is the one who has the authority to say, "Come forth," and he had to show up. I'll tell you a truth, I've got to close the door. I've got business to attend. My child is dead, my house is up for sale, I've lost my job, I've lost my husband, I'm about to lose my mind, and all you could do is stand up here to gaze and gossip. Excuse me, I gotta have a word with the alpha. I need to hear from the throne. I don't need any ifs, ands, or buts. It's time to close the door.

Elisha began to pray and intercede. He began to stretch, and as he began to stretch, the child began to sneeze, and as he began to sneeze, he began to get warm. As he began to get warm, he began to revive, and his life was restored.

I'm here to let you know that if you need restoration, just hand over your situation. No matter what it is, close the door and turn your eyes upon Jesus. Elisha could not have cared less about the size of the crowd. He was on a mission, so he closed the door. Excuse me, but this doesn't concern you. I'll see you in a bit, but right now, it is time close the door. This one is on God.

I remember once when I was invited to a meeting. I was taken into another room, and the door was closed. The host of the meeting insisted that the door had to be closed, as what was being discussed was of a confidential nature. As the meeting progressed, I understood why the door had to be closed.

Wisdom allows for doors to be closed sometimes to preserve character and integrity, for evidential purposes, and for privacy. At certain establishments you may see a Do Not Disturb sign or a sign that indicates the area is restricted, simply because those behind it do not wish to be interrupted. They are in need of total focus, so get the memo. Off limits. Check me later.

It is of utmost importance that we understand the intricacies of the supernatural because the Bible says that Elijah went up the stairs, closed the door, and lay on the lad mouth to mouth, eye to eye, and hand to hand and stretched himself. Can you imagine if the door wasn't closed and Elijah was seen on that young man in a time like this when everyone was suspicious of everything? *What* did the man of God do? By the time as the church people were done with Elisha, there would have been nothing in the world other than the blood of Jesus that would have been able to clear him.

I am sorry to inform you that the church has some of the most cantankerous people on earth. They lie, and they carry news (gossip). Sometimes they will bust up a good thing and even extinguish the fire of the Holy Ghost if they can get away with it. They then wipe their mouths clean and call it Christian practice. Elisha knew who some of them were. He learned from past mistakes. He learned to close the door.

You will notice as you carefully scan various scriptures that on several occasions, doors had to be closed for God to do a work. Small-minded persons today are under the impression that a closed door is an insult or means no access. But maturity will say otherwise because a closed door is not an insult, nor does it mean no access all the time. Sometimes it simply demonstrates order, control, authority, security, assurance, and perhaps patience.

How would you like to be undressed in the doctor's office when someone bursts through the door? The person does not say anything, but his or her actions speak untold volumes. You would become highly offended. Or if you were sitting on a toilet and someone walked in, you would probably become outraged and frustrated.

> And they laughed him to scorn. But when he had put them all out, he taketh the father and the mother of the damsel, and them that were with him, and entereth in where the damsel was lying. (Mark 5:40 KJV)

In Matthew 9:23–25 (KJV), a maid was dead. Jesus said to the multitude, "Give me a little space, for she is not dead." Shallow minds would have laughed Him to scorn. But when they were put outside, He closed the door and took her by the hand, and she arose. The door had to be closed.

It is amazing to see what can happen behind closed doors. Many people believe because a door is closed, there is some secret or an illegal activity going on. But I'll have you to know that the Bible says in Proverbs 27:3a, "For as a he thinketh in his heart, so is he." Just because you know who you are doesn't mean everyone is the same. Some people's minds are just corrupt and nasty.

This is why Jesus said in John 10:9, "I am the door." In other words, behind this door is the holy of holies, and this is where the Trinity is in full operation. You cannot just barge through. There is order. There are also two sides to every door, inside and outside. Which side are you?

Matthew 25:10 (KJV) says, "And while they went to buy, the bridegroom came; and they that were ready went in with him to the marriage: and the door was shut." The bridegroom came in, and the door was shut. Those standing on the outside could only imagine what was going on behind closed doors. They were celebrating and rejoicing in reunion. I want to encourage one and all to get onboard the old ship of Zion and close the door. There is safety when the door is closed. There is surety behind closed doors.

> After Noah put who and what God told him to put in the ark, according to Genesis 7:16 (KJV),
>
> "And they that went in, went in male and female of all flesh, as God had commanded him: and the Lord shut him in."

God Himself closed the door. The reason God closed the door is because when He does something, no human can undo it. Noah might have let in some friends or officials, but God closed the door.

On the outside of a closed door, you are open to almost anything. You are in dangerous territory. You are not guaranteed safety! You very well might not be accounted for. So why not just close the door to uncertainties?

Close the door to the spirit of anger and frustration.

Close the door to the spirit of jealousy and insecurity.

Close the door to the spirit of inconsistency and intimidation.

Close the door to the spirit of lousiness and pettiness.

Close the door to the spirit of lies, gossip, and malice.

Close the door to the spirit of hypocrisy, envy, and hatred.

Advise your friends and loved ones that there is no love lost, but you have decided to close the door on all the negativities in your past. Tell them you are about to close the door on some of them if they don't straighten up and fly right. Sometimes you have to close the door on friends and family.

Tell them how happy you are since the door has been closed, what a life change and an experience it has been. What a privilege it is to be able to close the door.

> And when thou art come in, thou shalt shut the door upon thee and upon thy sons, and shalt pour out into all those vessels, and thou shalt set aside that which is full.
>
> So she went from him, and shut the door upon her and upon her sons, who brought the vessels to her; and she poured out.
>
> And it came to pass, when the vessels were full, that she said unto her son, Bring me yet a vessel. And he said unto her, There is not a vessel more. And the oil stayed.
>
> Then she came and told the man of God. And he said, Go, sell the oil, and pay thy debt, and live thou and thy children of the rest. (2 Kings 4:4–7 KJV)

Tell them behind closed doors is where you have a spring of oil. You have oil to sell and to live on. According to this passage, there are riches behind closed doors. Tell them that behind closed doors, sickness, diseases, and witchcraft cannot overtake you.

Let folks know that you are exercising your rights as a citizen of the commonwealth of heaven. As it says in Isaiah 54:17 (KJV), "No weapon that is formed against thee shall prosper; and every tongue that shall rise against thee in judgment thou shalt condemn. This is the heritage of the servants of the Lord, and their righteousness is of me, saith the Lord."

Come and go with me. You won't regret it. There is freedom behind closed doors. Victory and life are behind closed doors. The deaf are hearing, the blind are receiving their sight, and folks are being raised from the dead behind closed doors. Tell them that your life depends on it! That is why it is necessary to close the door. Burdens are being lifted. All you do, brothers and sisters, is to recognize when it is time to close the door.

CHAPTER 3

Cultivating Faith: What Is Faith?

Hebrews 11:1(KJV)

Now faith is the substance of things hoped for, the evidence of things not seen.

Matthew 17:20 (KJV)

And Jesus said unto them, Because of your unbelief: for verily I say unto you, If ye have faith as a grain of mustard seed, ye shall say unto this mountain, Remove hence to yonder place; and it shall remove; and nothing shall be impossible unto you.

We look at Hebrews 11 as the faith chapter. But in reality, the entire Bible is the faith book. Hebrews 11:1 says that faith is the substance of things hoped for and the evidence of things not seen. Let me explain. Faith is a positive response to what grace has already made available. In other words, faith is the supernatural access through Christ to retrieve and bring to maturity what has already been approved. It is the promise and finished work of Christ.

Faith, like any other seed, has to be planted in good soil and nurtured before you can get a harvest. Faith needs something to work with. It needs the steps listed below to be in place.

1. The seed itself is the Word of God, sown into a clean heart and a pure mind, with no hate malice, envy, or jealousy.
2. It must then be processed by hope, patience, studying, and spending time in the Word.

You don't need to look for the promise of God, but because of the lack of knowledge, many cannot benefit from them.

Faith has nothing to do with the manifestation of God in anyone's life. But the manifestation of God depends totally on your faith. It is all about the individual. Jesus had difficulties getting anything done for people who did not have any faith. Let us look at Mark 6:5–6 (KJV): "And he could there do no mighty work, save that he laid his hands upon a few sick folks, and healed them.

And he marvelled because of their unbelief. And he went round about the villages, teaching."

There is no word, no knowledge, no belief, no faith, and no manifestation.

Your faith will put God to work. What we see is the manifestation. I really want to ask you a question: What do you have to work with? What are you providing for Jesus to work with? We need to stop looking for excuses and start planting. Some people utilize excuses and complaining as a career.

As believers in Christ, we have to rid ourselves of the denominational gods and beliefs and start searching for the universal God. Get busy planting! Stop running to people for what God Himself is not going to do because He has given you instructions to carry it out. In Matthew 8:2–3 it says, "And, behold, there came a leper and worshipped him, saying, Lord, if thou wilt, thou canst make me clean.

And Jesus put forth his hand, and touched him, saying, I will; be thou clean. And immediately his leprosy was cleansed."

Faith will automatically cancel all the ifs, the buts, the maybes, and the ands.

Faith stops, however, when you do not know the will of God.

Faith has no limit, time, or season. Faith is, according to Acts 1:7 (KJV), "And he said unto them, It is not for you to know the times or the seasons, which the Father hath put in his own power."

Matthew 17:20–21 says, "And Jesus said unto them, Because of your unbelief: for verily I say unto you, If ye have faith as a grain of mustard seed, ye shall say unto this mountain, Remove hence to yonder place; and it shall remove; and nothing shall be impossible unto you. Howbeit this kind goeth not out but by prayer and fasting."

Faith is once again explained in Matthew 13:31(KJV), "Another parable put he forth unto them, saying, The kingdom of heaven is like to a grain of mustard seed, which a man took, and sowed in his field."

He was referring to the size and what it could do.

The word *faith* is translated from the Greek word *pistils,* meaning conviction or firm persuasion. In Greek mythology, Pistis was the personification of good faith, trust, and reliability. In Christianity and in the New Testament, *pistis* is the word for faith. The Roman equivalent was *fides,* a personified concept that was significant in Roman culture.[1]

You can say that faith is our response to the mind of Christ, which is revealed to the saint through the Holy Spirit so that they can operate in or exercise dominion.

What is dominion? Some people call it control. Some people call it sovereignty. But it is a divine, God-given ability to reach beyond the natural realm and to believe the unreasonable. This was what God gave to humankind in the beginning to rule or dominate the earth and not each other. So, faith went to the left field or depreciated. According to Genesis 1:26–28, we must also bear in mind that faith is necessary for the future, the present, and the past. Let me explain:

> The Future: Why the future first? Because we were born with purpose or a list of expectations. Expectation speaks of something to come, so we all have to get the seed of faith planted and nurtured in us through the Word.
>
> The Present: Now that the Word/knowledge has been planted or sown in your hearts, and it is understood, then comes the process to correctly

---

[1] Strong, James. *Strong's Exhaustive Concordance of the Bible.* Nashville, TN: Abingdon Press, 1890.

apply what was understood. This exposes wisdom before manifestation is experienced.

The Past: What you have already done in your preparatory stages will cause God to bring your hopes and dreams into the now. However, just because you have in your possession what you asked for does not necessarily mean you can keep it. You are not out of the woods. Faith must now be sustained so you can hold the title deed for what you've been hoping for, which is the evidence.

Hope is always futuristic, but faith provides the confirmation.

The discussion does not question hope but hoped (v. 1), which is past tense.

Faith is always a *now* according to Hebrews 11:1. Faith has the ability to break down time barriers by supernaturally combining the past with the future, resulting in immediate manifestation.

In Mark 10:43, blind Bartimaeus received his sight immediately. In Acts 3:7, the lame man received strength in his feet immediately. There are many scriptures that support this claim. Once faith is activated, miracles, signs, and wonders are instantaneously downloaded.

Faith is the most important component in the world because faith is what puts the Holy Spirit to work. It takes faith to move God. According to Hebrews 11:6, our relationship and existence with God depend totally on faith. This faith ensures our victory over the enemy (James 2:20), but it comes with works.

Faith has the characteristics of Jesus Christ or the personality of God Himself. It comes and is developed or matured in a believer once he or she dedicates much time to studying the Bible, praying, and meditating (Romans 10:17).

By faith we understand that the worlds were framed by the Word of God so that the things that are seen were not made of the things that are visible but by the spoken Word of God, *"Let there be!"* (Genesis 1).

There is one faith with several dimensions:

- a faith for the promises of God (Abraham)
- a faith in the midst of trials and diversity (David, Noah, Daniel)

But faith itself is a seed that must be planted if you are expecting a harvest.

Belief is the source of reason and the raw material for commitment, persistence, and faithfulness. So when one loses that belief, then there is no explanation to life. I was once told that if you don't know where you are going, any road will indeed get you there.

Regardless of what you lose in life, never lose your faith!

The culture of heaven is love, the atmosphere is hope, and its currency is faith. It clearly indicates throughout the Bible that faith is necessary to function from a supernatural perspective.

Faith is the process of bringing to earth the manifestation of the finished work of Jesus. The mysteries of life will always make room for faith. All the provisions were made already.

In every country there is a special currency we use to

provide most physical necessities or to achieve certain materialistic properties. This currency is approved by the government of that country and is recognized or called legal tender. This means that it's okay for that country to spend it or use it in exchange for goods and services in that particular country. Without it, you may be considered poor, broke, or helpless.

You must know the will of God for faith to come. The Bible says it comes to you.

However, faith is the only currency that is valid to acquire anything from the country of heaven. All you need is enough.

The reality of the money most people risk their lives to gain is the same way. All you need is enough. Most people get out of bed with a big money agenda. We need to get out of bed with the understanding that faith is more worthwhile than money.

Faith must be obtained to freely function in both the physical and the supernatural world.

We oftentimes hear the phrase that money answer all things (Ecclesiastes 10:19). But I wonder if anyone know what that means. I say this because you can have money and not have faith, but when you have faith, you have money or the access to it.

Faith can also be considered "sure hope," which gives the believer access to all the rights, privileges, and benefits of the contents of the kingdom of God. Matthew 16:19 says, "And I will give you the keys to the kingdom of Heaven, and whatever you bind on earth will be bound in Heaven, and whatever you loose on earth will be loosed in Heaven."

This brings us to the importance of understanding that

faith must be a lifestyle and not a talk or a show. When faith is initiated, those who have it will be able to obtain anything the kingdom has to offer.

There are several things that keep faith from bringing hope to manifestation, and it is found in Proverbs 6:2, 18b. Talkative people and other people can't keep anything. They have to spread it like a wild forest fire.

> These six things doth the Lord hate: yea, seven are an abomination unto him:
>
> A proud look, a lying tongue, and hands that shed innocent blood,
>
> An heart that deviseth wicked imaginations, feet that be swift in running to mischief,
>
> A false witness that speaketh lies, and he that soweth discord among brethren. Proverbs 6:16–19 KJV)

One must also understand the laws of faith. There are twelve of them, and they are found in Hebrews 11:

1. The Law of Existence: You must believe that God is. He's active with regard to you personally.
2. The Law of Endurance: You must be prepared to wait patiently until God's time and purposes are fulfilled.
3. The Law of Just Providence: You must believe that He rewards those who diligently seek Him.
4. The Law of the Invisible: You must be prepared to believe in things beyond the experience of your senses, in things that have never happened before.

5. The Law of Heavenly Ambitions: Faith is directed into God's purposes and to God's ends and cannot function properly if it is focused on the here and now. Faith seeks the city that is to come.

6. The Law of Possibility: All things are possible with God.

7. The Law of Renunciation: Faith separates. It renounces all that is not faith, grasping on to God's purposes only.

8. The Law of Conquest: External is conquering. It does not submit to circumstances.

9. The Law of Reliance on Rhema: Abraham believed God's personal rhema word to him, and it was counted to him as righteousness.

10. The Law of Incomplete Knowledge: Abraham went out not knowing where he was going.

11. The Law of Assured Conviction: The ability to see the mountain-sized problem as a mere acorn in God's hand and to acknowledge that you have the answer with certainty.

12. The Law of Future Preparation: You must believe that God is working on your behalf in advance.

Faith encourages one to stay in the will of God. When you are in the will of God, you know His will for your life. There are two major enemies of faith: fear and doubt.

They are both related. They can both be sown into the mind by what you hear or see. In the presence of doubt and fear, it'll suggest that faith is absent. According to 2 Timothy 1:7, "For God did not give us the spirit of fear but of love and of a sound mind." Faith has no fear of trials, knows no limit, commits to the future, and is purified by testing. So we discover that our faith is only as strong as the tests it survives. The fuel to faith is testing.

As children of God, faith shapes our view of the world and guides our decisions. It outlasts every weapon that comes against it.

Faith is a belief in God that stands up to service whether God acts or not. Faith believes in the midst of God's silence. Will you worship in the midst of His silence?

Today many trust and depend solely on their talents and their abilities to accomplish a thing. But faith is the key to life and the key through life because faith sustains us.

Take-Home Points

- Faith is the currency to heaven.
- Build your faith by studying and meditating on the Word of God.
- Avoid fear and doubt.

CHAPTER 4

Remove the Stone and See the Glory

John 11:30–40 (KJV)

Now Jesus was not yet come into the town, but was in that place where Martha met him.

The Jews then which were with her in the house, and comforted her, when they saw Mary, that she rose up hastily and went out, followed her, saying, She goeth unto the grave to weep there.

Then when Mary was come where Jesus was, and saw him, she fell down at his feet, saying unto him, Lord, if thou hadst been here, my brother had not died.

When Jesus therefore saw her weeping, and the Jews also weeping which came with her, he groaned in the spirit, and was troubled.

And said, Where have ye laid him? They said unto him, Lord, come and see.

Jesus wept.

Then said the Jews, Behold how he loved him!

And some of them said, Could not this man, which opened the eyes of the blind, have caused that even this man should not have died?

Jesus therefore again groaning in himself cometh to the grave. It was a cave, and a stone lay upon it.

Jesus said, Take ye away the stone. Martha, the sister of him that was dead, saith unto him, Lord, by this time he stinketh: for he hath been dead four days.

Jesus saith unto her, Said I not unto thee, that, if thou wouldest believe, thou shouldest see the glory of God?

The time will come when it seems like life has taken a turn for the worse. Your seasons seem to be dried up. You have been forgotten, rejected, and denied. It appears as if you're always the one to inherit the short end of the stick! You may wonder whether God has failed you because of the cards life has dealt and devastating experiences you constantly encounter. I have come to share the good news to all and sundry. Come what may, all is well!

God wants you to know He's God in the beginning, God in the middle, and God in the end. He's saying to remind you of His infinite power and that He's God almighty all by Himself. You need to know,"

Being confident of this very thing, that he which hath begun a good work in you will perform it until the day of

Jesus Christ." (Philippians 1:6 KJV). God has never changed His mind about the thoughts He's laid out for you in Jeremiah 29:11(KJV): "For I know the thoughts that I think toward you, saith the Lord, thoughts of peace, and not of evil, to give you an expected end."

So today, many just need to see Him for who He is. Know Him in the power of His resurrection and in the fellowship of His suffering. We need to trust every day!

> I am reminded of a song by Edgar Page Stiles that says, "Trusting through the stormy way, even when your way seems small, trusting Jesus, that is all."

Just remove the stone and discover that there's hope and life on the other side. Some people happen to be the stone in their own lives. They have hard hearts and a disabled comprehension or inability to understand what God is saying. They have become a hindrance to themselves. Another reason some will never experience a move of God is because of their poor attitude, and let me tell you something about a poor attitude. It is like trying to bail the ocean dry with a teaspoon. Impossible. But until comprehension is achieved and the stone is rolled away, nothing is gonna happen.

I suggest to you that there are some things God can do for you and some things that He cannot do for you. I draw reference to Matthew 10:8. This tells you that whatever God command *you* to do, He'll never do. God will never turn around and carry out His own instructions. Some people are known for reverse psychology. A lack of knowledge and a lack of understanding are two of the deadliest components that anyone could ever encounter. It is an open invitation to fatal consequences!

Jesus was a family friend to Lazarus, Mary, and Martha. It happened that Lazarus had died. This placed Him in a sort of precarious position. I can tell you from personal experience about being in certain positions. It can put you in any number of situations, whereby your friendship or your office could be compromised or put under heavy scrutiny. Some people may not even like you, but they know who you are and what you are capable of. So, they hang on to you as a point of reference. They will tolerate you until they have accomplished their goal.

Then you will experience their true colors. As it is said in the Bahamas, "True character is understood in serious circumstances."

Your office can put you in situations sometimes where you can't be decisive. You do not want to hurt or offend anyone. It can place a sense of responsibility on you, making you feel obligated or answerable to folks. When you cannot respond right away to their situation's requests, it compromises or paralyzes their expectation of you, and you're now discovering why they were with you in the first place. This is how Lazarus's family felt to some degree about Jesus, but this was not the case. Thank God He's not petty and irresponsible.

Jesus, after consultation with the Father, communicated to His disciples that Lazarus was (asleep) dead. He explained that his death was temporary and that He was going to Bethany to awake him out of his sleep. He showed up four days later. I thank God for Jesus, because while we were yet sinners, He died for us. Whatever our present concerns are, it has already been addressed on our behalf. *Father, I thank You that You have heard my prayer.*

When Jesus arrived, there were mixed emotions or mixed feelings among the people, as some would say. Some folks were angry, some folks were happy, some folks were envious, some were sad, and some could not even care. There was total confusion, large crowds everywhere spectating, speculation, and a whole heap of gossiping going on.

They were not looking for anything. They were just there to see what was going on so they could have a word to gossip to a friend that afternoon. They may blow up the social media and pick you to pieces over Sunday dinner when they get home. In the process, they are missing out on the move of God. Unfortunately, they are living their everyday lives from a hopeless perspective. This leaves them worse than the man at the pool of Bethesda, just an unnecessary factor. He was hanging around the pool for so long that he lost focus on his purpose for being there. He started hallucinating and finding excuses when the question was asked, *"Will thou be made whole?"* (See John 5:6.)

The family expected Jesus to move right away. (Lazarus is dead. We saw You open the eyes of the blind. We saw You turn water into wine. We saw You make the lame to walk. We saw You raise Jairus's daughter. Now it's our time, and You're showing up four days late. What are You going to do? Why were You not here?)

I am always reminded that familiarity usually breathes contempt. They had no idea that this was an orchestrated, divine act of God, so the attitude was on. They began to show their true colors. Typical folks—when they cannot get the best of you and cannot control you, then all of a sudden you are a problem and you are not necessary.

They didn't know that Jesus was in the process of being glorified. They didn't know miracles were being birthed, because not only was Lazarus being raised from the dead but the trend of thought for many would be changed and they would believe and be converted. This was a high moment in the spirit realm. Can you imagine history, which was about to be recorded? There was a revival in the graveyard, a place where only the dead are disposed of, and all of a sudden, the grave is about to give birth. And all you can talk about is where was He for four days?

Who cares about what your thoughts are? Yes, it's four days later. Yes, I am your friend, and according to you I am late. But if you believe in Me, though he's been dead, yet shall he live, because I am the resurrection. In other words, true life travels with Me, and when I show up, death has to return life to its victim and render him alive. Sickness has to return vitality to your bones and render you healthy. Sorrow has to return joy to its victims and render them happy. Poverty has to return wealth to you because I'm on the scene. I did not show up to make up the number. I showed up to make a difference. In fact, I am the difference. When you remove the stone, you'll begin to experience the life I intended for you to live.

Sometimes narrow mindedness and limited foresight can cause an individual to miss out on the bigger picture. I've also learned the danger of sharing big dreams with small-minded people. Joseph too was in that category (see Genesis 37–50).

Both Mary and Martha, in their communication to Jesus, in verses 21 and 32 indicated that had He been there, this catastrophe would not have been in question. But His response to them was, "I am the resurrection and the life." In other words, there is no death in My DNA.

This is why I gave credit to the prodigal son. He was smart. He asked for his portion, even though he blew every dime. He knew his father could not die while the other brother was waiting for something to be read in the graveyard.

Jesus was explaining to them that His very purpose for dying was that as many as believed in Him, He would revoke the penalty of death and give them the power to become sons of God (John 1:12). They would also have life more abundantly.

So many would not be able to get a breakthrough because of their mediocre thoughts and their inability to believe and to trust in God. I can concur with the writer and only imagine what he must have been going through as he tearfully sat down and penned the song, "'Tis so sweet to trust in Jesus, just to take Him at His word, just to rest upon His promise, just to know thus said the Lord."

He took Jesus at His word, satisfied and settled on His promises because he knew what it meant to trust him.

Jesus is now on the scene. He heard everyone. He saw everything. Then He ordered them to take Him to the place where they buried Lazarus. He was at the graveyard. When Jesus is on the scene, something great is about to happen. He further instructed them to remove the stone. They began to reason amongst themselves, "Well by now he stinks. It's useless. It's too late. This is four days later." Today all you need to do is shut your mouth, stop the bickering, and remove the stone. Stop putting your personal conclusions to other people's potentials and abilities. This is why I keep reiterating the consequences of the inability to understand. After all that I've said to you, what are you talking about? Just stand still and see the salvation of the Lord.

Once the stone is removed, the rest will be up to Jesus. You will see the power and the glory of God. Because according to you, Lazarus is dead. According to you, the situation is over. According to you, the final chapter has been read already. *News break:* I am not here to operate based on your guesses and expectations. I am here to show you that there is life behind that stone. You all had a plan for who or what was behind the stone, but God had a purpose.

Too many times folks allow other people to determine their destiny and render them lifeless, made them feel unworthy, useless, and good for nothing. But if you can subpoena Jesus to the graveyard, your dreams, hope, future, families, marriage, finances, and health will come alive. When you roll away your stone, you will discover everything you thought was dead has come alive and is well. The Bible says when the Son has set you free, you are free indeed. He alone can revive your potential, your focus, and your purpose. You can live life to the fullest and with great expectations.

Sometimes, you have to recognize the powerless, unnecessary, and unfruitful people around you. Start severing some ties. You have to delete that negative perpetrator. Break away from the social network. Abort some places and things because if you don't, they will definitely force you into being another statistic like themselves. Some people are nothing but stumbling blocks and blessing hijackers, and if they are stumbling blocks to themselves, can you imagine what they'll do to you? These are times to fly high. Stop hanging with chickens and be the eagle you were called to be.

They'll run you up on brakes. Sit back and laugh because their mission has been accomplished. Their attitude is keeping them from being successful, so they don't want to see you succeed either. But thank God for being who He is because, if you mind some of them, you'll be brought down to nothing and won't even know how it happened. But I want to encourage you today to adapt to a change in life for the better. Don't entertain people with a corrupt mindset. Stand strong, hold your heads up high, and focus on the essentials. He's not the God of a second chance as we were led to believe but of another chance. He continually gives us chances.

Some of your future has been bound up, shut up, and buried for dead behind the stone, never to be heard of again. But Jesus is here today. You have an obligation to roll away the stone. It is a guarantee you'll be yourself. All your disappointments will become appointments. Your tears of sorrows will become tears of joy. Your dark nights will be illuminated into daylight. The Bible says that the blessings of the Lord will overtake you. Psalm 23 says goodness and mercies will follow you for sure. You will know your purpose, and you will pursue it successfully.

When your stone is removed, your potential will be exposed. What was limited will be limitless. What used to confuse you will not any longer. You will receive clarity. You will know that the sky is not your limit but God is. This is when Jesus can cater to your circumstances, to your situations, whatever they maybe, and say *come forth. It's resurrection time.* Loose him/her. Let them go free.

No government, no grave, and no church clique can hold you back when the resurrection says, "Come forth."

Many potentials, dreams, and great ideas have been buried by the dictates of society. Folks have allowed how people feel about them to paralyze their potentials and put purpose to a standstill. They cannot handle the truth and do not like your style. So they go around to poison the minds of others against the innocent. I must say that God hates wickedness. He is angry with the wicked every day. If God be for you, tell me who can be against you? So stop trying to funeralize things that have resurrection potential. And roll the stony hearts away.

The woman with the issue of blood had to remove the stone of fear. The man on the road to Jericho had to remove the stone of hopelessness. Naaman removed the stone of pride. The Shunamite woman removed the stone of frustration. The blind man removed the stone of disbelief. Today you and I are not different. Stop looking for recognition. Get the stone of ignorance, poor self-esteem, and incompetence out of the way. You will never be recognized until you're organized.

Jesus is still in the graveyard, still asking you to remove the stone of wickedness, envy, hatred, false accusations, and greed so you can experience the power of God. Get rid of the derogatory mindset and unnecessary comments about your neighbor, and stop trying to drum up evil and discord in the house of God, looking for company to destroy other people's character without a reason. They always see the fault in everyone but themselves. Don't let them get you in the mix of unnecessary and fruitless chattering. I can tell you that they don't wish you well either. It is only a matter of time before you become their next victim, because hurting people usually seek to hurt people. Their desire for you is that you be a failure just like them. They will watch you ride into a most miserable sunset.

It is time to get real. Rule out the counterfeit. David invited the Lord to search him, know him, try him, and see if there be any wicked ways in him. He needed the stone to be rolled away before he could be led to the path everlasting. In the midst of all that God is doing in the lives of His people, there are still folks who will never satisfy, refuse to understand, still can't love their neighbor, don't know how to share, still carry around unforgiveness in their hearts, and who hate on you and can't even say why. But if you have the true love of Christ in your hearts, you'll do otherwise. I am reminded in Proverbs 22:24–25 to make no friendship with an angry person and not to go anywhere with a furious person, or else you'll adopt their ways. Some folks just do not love themselves. So why are you expecting them to love you? Get over it! They did not like Jesus.

I came to tell you about this man. He sticks closer than a brother. This friend is still in the resurrection business. He is waiting to resurrect you from every dead situation, no matter how long, no matter the condition. His name is Jesus, and when you do your part and remove the stone, you'll see the glory of God.

This invitation is extended to all. "Come unto me, all ye that are labored and are heavy laden and I will give you rest" (Matthew 28:11). "Come, let us reason together says the Lord, though your sins be red as crimson, they shall be as white as snow, though they be red as scarlet, they shall be as wool" (Isaiah 1:18–19).

Although you may be bound and engulfed by naysayers, unwell wishers, and hypocrites, He's still vested with resurrection power. What He's opened no person can close, and what He's closed no person can open. He is saying to remove the stone. Come forth, loose him, and let him go.

Today, you remove the stone out of your way and allow Jesus to do a great and mighty work in you and through you, in Jesus's name.

CHAPTER 5

Understanding Your Mandate

First of all, a mandate is an order or authorization to do something, whether or not it is legal. In its simplest form, a mandate is an assignment. When the word *mandate* is accurately processed, the individual will also arrive at the following steps, which are necessary steps to achieve your mandate: vision, preparation, purpose, focus, accountability, and management.

> Vision: This is the ability to think about or plan the future with imagination or wisdom. This also includes the ability to listen and discern visions, ideas, and thoughts. However, one's inner voice, when assessed properly, will initiate a communication between the speaker and the listener (prayer). Once the communication is visualized, this process will be the driving force of vision to the other characteristics of the mandate.

Preparation: It's impossible to receive a mandate without preparation. It's impossible to receive a mandate from God or a person without first having been made aware of what it is, what it entails, who is giving it, and how it is to be executed. Preparation is, however, one of the most important aspects of becoming successful. As we see in Genesis 1, nothing was initiated by God before preparation was in place. Without preparation, you're a failure already.

Purpose: This is the original reason for the function of a thing being created. Purpose is actually the mold for vision because it designs and initiates the cultivation for the mandate.

Focus: This is the ability to saturate oneself in the interest and with clarity.

Accountability: This is the ability to take charge or be able to account to someone else for your assignment in detail.

Management: This is to properly control, maintain, and deliver or distribute to whomever, wherever, and whatever is included in your mandate.

Once each aspect is clearly comprehended, you should not experience any difficulties in adherence or execution. This brings humankind to the forefront of the mandate itself. It is transparent in Matthew 28:18–20 and Mark 16:15. As I pondered and meditated on both scripture verses for many years, I discovered that they are the hinges that link humankind to the blessings of God. Deuteronomy 28:1–14 specifically explains the benefits of our mandate. Our mandate is to obey the voice of God as in the execution of the great commission.

Actually understanding your mandate and not putting it into practice is sin (James 4:17). In reality, the equation is very simple. There are folks who find themselves in a seesaw predicament because they are leaning to their own understanding. They fail to be fully committed to God and to the given mandate. So they end up tolerating a lot of things and are expecting something to change. Matthew 11:15, Revelation 2:29, and Mark 4:9, 23 say, "He who has an ear, let him hear."

CHAPTER 6

What Are You Doing about Your Mandate?

Romans 10:1–3

Brethren, my heart's desire and prayer to God for Israel is, that they might be saved. For I bear them record that they have a zeal of God, but not according to knowledge. For they being ignorant of God's righteousness, and going about to establish their own righteousness, have not submitted themselves unto the righteousness of God

Today the world is experiencing a lot of turmoil, and this is driving many to confusion and crisis. You may have noticed an escalation in criminal activities in your neighborhood, such as murder, armed robberies, rape, burglary, and domestic violence, among other unnatural societal issues.

With a closer observation, you will understand that the world itself is vividly evolving into a specialized conglomerate of evils, but humans are working tirelessly to find ways and means to resolve these pressing issues. I humbly submit to you today that the way that seems right is successfully taking root in the house of God, right before our very presence, and the watchmen are almost sleep.

All the technical paraphernalia, the intellectual eloquence, and other sophistication wouldn't be able to eradicate the spiritual fatality that's forthcoming. There are dark clouds of negativities, destruction, and disaster hovering over us, awaiting the first opportunity to disperse fire and brimstone on us, and we don't want to say a thing about it. However, it seems like the more things change, the more they will remain the same, and I can assure you that for this epidemic to be defused, it's necessary that you execute your God-given mandate.

> Ye worship ye know not what: we know what we worship: for salvation is of the Jews. (John 4:22 KJV)

> Hear the word of the Lord, ye children of Israel: for the Lord hath a controversy with the inhabitants of the land, because there is no truth, nor mercy, nor knowledge of God in the land. By swearing, and lying, and killing, and stealing, and committing adultery, they break out, and blood toucheth blood. (Hosea 4:1–2 KJV)

Jesus flipped the script, and now some may go through the water and some through the flood, but all this morning must go.

Whether we believe it or not, the foundation of every evil, be it word, thought, or deed, is sin. The Bible says that all unrighteousness is indeed sin, and so, the question is, How do we address it? What's the solution? I'll tell you. Seriously get on your knees and bombard the portals of heaven. Empty yourself of every impurity. Tell God how long you've been pretending and joking in the house. Tell Him how you've been a grave all your life, and ask Him to create a clean heart and renew a right spirit in you. Ask Him to allow you to see the filthy and crooked life you been living over the years that you've allowed yourself to believe is okay. Ask him to give you another chance to repent and sail the wild seas no more.

Romans 10:13 says, "For whosoever shall call upon the name of the Lord shall be saved." My question is, How do you believe? How do you call upon the name of the Lord? Read a little further. You'll see a number of important questions that not many have taken the time to understand. These are questions that will formulate supernatural equilibrium so you'll know whether you are effectively carrying out your mandate.

> How then shall they call on him in whom they have not believed and how shall they believe in Him of whom they have not heard and how shall they hear without a preacher? And how shall they preach except they be sent? (Romans 13:14–15)

Your mandate, however, is to distinguish your purpose and successfully execute it in a timely manner. God requires nothing more, nothing less.

I'm wondering if it is so simple to say, "Believe in the Lord Jesus Christ," or "Call on the name of the Lord and thou shall be saved." But it's so difficult to happen. These prerequisites are indeed factual, but they will never take effect unless order is put into perspective. Do you realize that all questions relating to the mandate of God are directed at the church? Have you ever wondered why? It is because His expectation of people is high. He expects people to be faithful, truthful, and obedient in righteousness. He's looking forward to people's productivity levels being at an all-time high.

The Bible says that many were called but few are chosen. This adds to the reason why there is so much disjunction in the church. Folks are taking it upon themselves to pursue other people's purposes and ending up on collision courses. Everywhere you go, everyone wants to lead and no one wants to follow. If you spend your life trying to be someone else or play someone else's role, when are you going to be you?

According to Genesis 1:26, leadership is given to all humankind, and trapped in every follower is a leader's perspective, and if you took the time to identify yourself, you would discover who you are. You'll know your purpose. Your life will have meaning, and function will follow suit. But the real struggle in the house is *power.*

For far too long, the church has been held hostage by spiritual dementors who are pretending to be saints who only come out to display the form of godliness. They look for prophecy, gossip and what they haven't lost, and they criticize the preacher because he didn't tell them what they wanted to hear. But I heard Paul in Colossians 3:1 saying, "If ye then be risen with Christ, seek those things which are above, where Christ is seated at the right hand of the God and set your affection on things above not on things on the earth." Ladies and gentlemen, believe it or not, your salvation might be at stake, and you will be held accountable for your actions. Get serious about your mandate.

It's time now for folks to stop making friends and be serious about making a difference. We must launch into the deep, and become real fishers of men. Many are not aware, but the church is almost in a state of disrepair because of lousy soldiers who don't have a clue about their duty. They have been given a mandate to execute and will therefore be faced with fatal consequences for a failure to deliver.

Isaiah 58:1 says, "Cry aloud, spare not, lift up your voice like a trumpet, and shew my people their transgression, and the House Of Jacob their sins."

Second Chronicles 7:14 says, "If my people, which are called by my name, shall humble themselves, pray, seek my face and turn from their wicked ways, then will I hear from Heaven, I'll forgive their sins, and will heal the land. Humble yourself under the mighty hand of God, that He may exalt you in due time." The question is, What are you doing about your mandate?

Internalize these questions:

- How do I know whether I've been called by God?
- Do I know my purpose?
- Have I totally surrendered everything to God?
- Do I know what my mandate entails?
- Am I studying to show myself approved unto God?

- Do I have the ability to recognize the voice of God and say for sure it is Him? This will definitely eliminate all doubts and inconsistencies.
- Am I spending time in prayer?
- Am I acknowledging God in all my ways?
- Am I making my ministry foolproof?
- What type of seeds am I sowing? Am I a liability or an asset to the kingdom of God?
- Am I meeting God's expectation?

Fellow saints, you must know your job description. There is no way on earth you can do a job you don't know the first thing about. You'll never be effective. Time is fading away. The coming of Christ will not be postponed because you have lost your bearings or are looking for one.

Saints of God, endeavor to press toward the mark, for the high calling in Jesus Christ. There are souls to rescue. This morning your mandate is your purpose, and your purpose is your mandate.

The claim everywhere is that God called me. He sent me, and you can't judge me. Have you ever noticed how the so-called saints pay little to no attention to the call they claim to have? You were called and chosen for a purpose. What are you doing about it?

This leads back to Matthew 7:22–23, where Jesus said, "Many will say to me on that day, Lord, haven't we prophesied in your name? And in your name, casted out devils, and done many wonderful works? And I will profess to them, I never knew you, depart from me you that work iniquity."

What am I saying? Those of you who are called were also

chosen for training and empowerment before going out to discipleship. One of the major responsibilities of a disciple is to learn the art of reproduction and to protect the flock from being scattered or harmed, not to have the sanctuary as a revolving door. Matthew 28:19 tells us to go therefore and make disciples of all nations, not friends. This doesn't include the saved but the lost (Luke 19:10).

The mandate for the church is set out in both Matthew 28:19 and Mark 16:15. The entire Bible is attached to those two verses, and preparation is essential. Training is a grave necessity. You must have 2 Timothy 2:15 down pat, and you must rely totally on the Holy Spirit. This is why the apostle Paul says in 2 Timothy 4:17, "Notwithstanding, the Lord stood with me, and strengthened me, that by me the preaching might be fully known, and that all the Gentiles might hear: and I was delivered out of the mouth of the lion." This suggests that we need the backing and the equipping of the Holy Spirit. Don't go if God didn't send you, because you'll be lined up for fatal consequences.

Your prayer and fasting life must be intact. Humility is a must. Timing and order are key. Wisdom, circumspection, sobriety, integrity, and your body presented as a living sacrifice are of vital importance. This usually happens on an empty stomach. Your mandate is crucial because it is the sole purpose for your existence.

Second Timothy 2:21 says, "If a man therefore purge himself from the impurities of sin, he shall be a vessel of honor, sanctified and meet for the Master's use, and prepared to every good work." When they couldn't perform certain tasks, the disciples asked why. Jesus told them this kind came by much fasting and prayer. To address this present epidemic, you'll have to increase your prayer and fasting. Empowerment doesn't just fall on anyone.

Faith is the greatest component. Information is the greatest tool. Wisdom and communication are the driving forces. This sums up the definition of *training*.

This is how you learn what and what not to do.

You will learn how not to get offended when truth is told.

You will learn how to die to self and learn servant leadership skills.

You will learn how to govern yourself.

You will learn not to oppose your allies.

You will learn to embrace the Word and not focus on the speaker.

You will learn how to lay aside every weight and the sin that so easily besets you.

You will learn not to sow seeds of discord in the body of Christ.

You will learn total forgiveness and eradicate the pettiness.

You will learn the beauty of coexistence. You will seek obedience and not perfection. Discipline yourself.

Spending time with God seems to be a crime among the Christians. Many don't want to humble themselves. They don't want to sacrifice, don't want to wait, don't have teachable spirits, and don't want anyone to tell them anything. I am saved. I don't need training. Just give me a microphone and an opportunity, and I'll show you exactly what a lack of knowledge is all about. This is what is killing the church.

All sorts of misquoted and incomplete scriptures mix up unbelievers and weak Christians. Frustration sets in, and you're at the mercy of ignorance. This is not how folks are drawn to Christ.

It's unthinkable to know there are experienced veterans sitting down in the congregation who are afraid to address biblical inconsistencies and afraid to correct these people. They are expecting things to change when they didn't. If you don't like your harvest, change your seed.

Titus 1:13 says, "This witness is true, rebuke them sharply that they may be sound in faith." We are afraid to rebuke people today in the house of God because we don't want to hurt people's feelings. We don't want to lose members or friends. I think when these things are enforced, folks won't just roll out of their beds and run out with stuff they dreamed about the previous night but will properly prepare themselves. When God gives you a vision, He has already made the provision.

Halfway information is a lie, it will put a bridle on purpose, and existence will be of no significance. When purpose is not known, abuse will become inevitable and ignorance will dominate. The eunuch claimed he needed someone to interpret the scripture. Could you imagine what would have happened if Philip hadn't been equipped?

In the time church people take to complain about membership and policies, they should be at the feet of Gamaliel, trying to find the purpose and will of God for their lives, while dismantling the spirit of pride and greed, learning to love their neighbors as themselves, and being extracted from the disparity they so frequently experience. Put on the whole armor of God so you may be productive.

If you allow the past to take a grip on the present, your future becomes redundant or unfruitful. Old things have passed away. Romans 8:1 (KJV) says, "There is therefore now, no condemnation to them which are in Christ Jesus, who walk not after the flesh, but after the Spirit. For the law of the Spirit of life in Christ Jesus has made you free." And as we know in John 8:36, "If the Son therefore shall make you free, ye shall be free indeed."

Who the Son sets free is guaranteed freedom!

So let go of your neighbor. Stop getting involved in things that aren't necessary. This morning the harvest is huge, but the laborers are few. Get those sleeves up because there is much to be accomplished. *What are you doing about your mandate?*

A mandate has been set before you and me. Our future depends on it. Our obedience will determine whether we will find eternal rest. Romans 11:29 says, "For the gifts and calling of God are without repentance." This is not a game. The question is asked in Hebrews 2:3, "How shall we escape?" It is required that we watch in all things, endure affliction, do the work of an evangelist, and make full use of our ministry. The question remains: *What are you doing about your mandate?*

Folks still need to know that there is hope. They don't need to hear about cars, husbands, and financial breakthroughs. What they need to know is Matthew 6:33. If you ever want to see a breakthrough, spend time in the Word. It's filled with prophecy.

Paul's fear was that Israel had a zeal for God, but not according to knowledge. This applies to the Bahamas. Many have a zeal for God but are allergic to the requirements. Someone needs to know that salvation exists and is necessary.

We need to know that the wage of sin is death. We need to know that Jesus cares and is still saying, "Come unto me all ye that are labored and are heavy laden and I will give you rest" (Matthew 11:28 KJV). He is still saying, "Come let us reason together." How are these people going hear this if you don't tell them? How can the captives be set free if you are confused about your mandate? This morning, do yourself a favor and check your mandate. Because a voice is still crying in the wilderness. Prepare ye the way of the Lord, and make His path straight.

We have much to accomplish.

John 9:4 says, "I must do the work of him who sent me, while it is day. Night is coming when no one can work."

Get off those phones, get off the back of those cars in the night, get out of the obese man's house, bridle your tongues, and stop the negative gossiping. This is what causes spiritual deterioration.

Turn your plates down, go to your neighbor and confess your faults, seek forgiveness, love one another, obey God in all things, and you'll know what do about your mandate.

CHAPTER 7

The Power of Prayer

James 5:17 (KJV)

Elias was a man subject to like passions as we are, and he prayed earnestly that it might not rain: and it rained not on the earth by the space of three years and six months.

Prayer is communication between God and people. It causes us to become better acquainted with him. Prayer is a gift from God and should not be taken lightly, as some do.

It is universal, meaning that everyone can do it. No matter what your nationality or language is, it's the same in the hearing of God once it's done the right way, and the more you practice it, the easier and more effective it becomes. Prayer is a ministry.

Even though the greatest component in life is faith, the greatest thing in life a Christian can do is to pray. And the most important lesson one can learn besides learning how to pray is learning how to apply it effectively.

When you learn how to pray effectively, you are then able

through faith to release God's power for your personal need and the need for others.

Philippians 4:19 says, "But my God shall supply all of your need according to his riches in glory by Christ Jesus."

Matthew 6:5–6 says, "As Jesus thought his disciples to pray, Our Father, He insisted that they reverenced God as Father, which art in Heaven, letting them know He is sovereign God of all and he reigns supreme from wherever He is."

Hallowed be thy name. Holy is His name. Thy kingdom come means God's will and purpose and God's nature show through in every state of affairs. Thy will be done in earth as it is in heaven means that the will of God should be carried out in earth as it is being done in heaven.

Give us our daily bread, meaning to daily provide comfort and support for us in this present world and forgive us our trespasses as we have forgiven those who have trespassed against us, meaning to forgive us for our transgressions (sin) or wrongdoing and lead us not into temptations, to not allow us to undergo more than we can bear, but deliver us from evil, meaning not to let the devil overcome you, for thine is the kingdom, the power, and the glory, forever. You hold eternal supremacy or authority over the universe and the heavens and earth because everything belongs to You. Amen.

He also taught them how not to be like the hypocrites who love to be seen and like showing off in crowds, in megachurches, and in public forums. But they need to embrace the privilege of their privacy so that the God who sees in secret will reward them openly.

Many today are strongly under the impression that talking loud is talking sense. I'll be the first to tell you that the devil is and has always been a liar. Ecclesiastes 5:3b states, "And a fool's voice is known by the multitude of words."

According to Luke 16:8, the Bible says that the children of this world are in their generation, wiser than the children of light. In plain words, they try to mislead or deceive others. They may not be saved and sanctified like you or me but they are not fools. So we find that the difference between the children of the world and the children of light is their prayer life. They don't know God, so they don't have one.

Jesus said in Matthew 6:2 (KJV), "Therefore when thou doest thine alms, do not sound a trumpet before thee, as the hypocrites do in the synagogues and in the streets, that they may have glory of men. Verily I say unto you, They have their reward."

Bear in mind that to pray is one thing and to pray in faith is another, because if we are to worship God, it must be in Spirit and in truth. "God is a Spirit: and they that worship him must worship him in spirit and in truth" (John 4:24 KJV).

When prayer and faith are combined, it initiates the supernatural miraculously and is capable of merging the past and the future with the present, to manifest in the now.

Proverbs 18:21 (KJV) says, "Death and life are in the power of the tongue: and they that love it shall eat the fruit thereof."

Words can only be spoken in communication either to the negative or to the positive, but when it is accompanied with faith, expect something to happen.

This is why the Bible says in Luke 18:1 (KJV), "And he spake a parable unto them to this end, that men ought always to pray, and not to faint."

It goes on further to Jeremiah 33:3 (KJV), which says, "Call [pray] to me and I will answer you and show you great and mighty things which you do not know."

Prayer just happens to be the channel or pipeline through which all blessings flow from God to humankind. This is how we receive healing, forgiveness, power, love, and the only way of knowing God.

Prayer is a privilege and should not be taken for granted. It is also a battleground whereby Satan can attack you. It is in the place of prayer where we engage the devil, only for him to discover that the victory has already been won for us at Calvary.

Prayer is a partnership, and the better you get at it, the more you learn that it is never alone.

At one point, God used to communicate with humanity directly, up until they decided to prove Him right by breaking the trust and obedience barrier between them both.

There are many things that makes prayer ineffective, including unforgiveness, doubt and instability, fear, selfishness, injustice, fault finding, complaining, judgment and criticism, lust, adultery, envy, holding grudges, jealousy, and wrong motives.

God communicates with people through several methods:

- He speaks through the scripture.
- He speaks through the church.
- He speaks through the Holy Spirit.
- He speaks through the prophets.
- He speaks through visions, dreams, direct revelations, and more.

Here are some effects of prayer:

- Prayer allows you to bear the stink of life.
- Prayer changes you.
- Prayer enables you to bear the burdens of others and your own burdens.
- Prayer brings joy to your life.
- Prayer allows you to get attuned to God's will.
- Prayer helps you not to enter into temptation.
- Prayer brings the blessing.
- Prayer brings healing.
- Prayer brings deliverance.

But the communication has not stopped. There are several aspects of prayer, but I just want to touch on a few

The center of prayer is God. You should not focus on your issues, or even other people's issues or needs. Put your focus on God. Loving Him, listening to Him, worshipping Him, obeying Him, and praising Him should be the heart of prayer. This makes prayer positive and powerful.

Prayer works because God answers. Prayer works because God is alive, and He loves everybody. God is a personal, living, loving Father who wants to do wonders through us and for us.

God's will is the goal of prayer. Prayer is saying yes to Him, letting Him set your desires. It is getting to know Him and understanding His will and purpose for your life.

Prayer is thanksgiving, gratitude, praise, and adoration. Prayer is a commitment. It is believing God, rejoicing in God, a contact with divine presence, and living communication with God. And only through prayer do we come into the experience of the living God.

Prayer governs conduct, and conduct decides character. You can operate smoothly in prayer when you know the will of God for your life.

Prayer is the most important weapon against trials, the most effective medicine against sickness and diseases, and the most valuable gift you can give to anyone.

Are you sick and heavy laden? Take it to the Lord in prayer.

Are you weary or heavy hearted? Take it to the Lord in prayer.

Did society destroy you and bury you, leaving you for dead? Take it to the Lord in prayer.

Is there trouble anywhere? Do not be discouraged. Take it to the Lord in prayer.

Did governments deny you and did friends turn their backs on you? Take it to the Lord in prayer.

When the devil desired to sift Peter like wheat (Luke 22:31–32), Jesus did not say to Peter, "I'll work a miracle or see what the people have got to say." He said, "But I have prayed for you that your faith fail not. And when you are converted, strengthen the rest." In other words, I'll defend you through the power of prayer.

James 5:16b (KJV) says, "The effectual fervent prayer of a righteous man availeth much."

Elijah prayed and prayers stopped the rain for three and an half years. Big prayer, big power; little prayer, little power; no prayer, no power. And that's the size of it.

Alan Jackson penned the words in his song, "What a friend we have in Jesus, all our sins and grief to bear, what a privilege to carry everything to God in prayer."

And now you know the importance of prayer. It develops our relationship with God and helps us to know Him more intimately. Use prayer to petition Him and impact the world around you, keeping an edge on the enemy.

CHAPTER 8

Living in the Overflow

Joel 2:23–27 (KJV)

Be glad then, ye children of Zion, and rejoice in the Lord your God: for he hath given you the former rain moderately, and he will cause to come down for you the rain, the former rain, and the latter rain in the first month. And the floors shall be full of wheat, and the vats shall overflow with wine and oil. And I will restore to you the years that the locust hath eaten, the cankerworm, and the caterpiller, and the palmerworm, my great army which I sent among you. And ye shall eat in plenty, and be satisfied, and praise the name of the Lord your God, that hath dealt wondrously with you: and my people shall never be ashamed. And ye shall know that I am in the midst of Israel, and that I am the Lord your God, and none else: and my people shall never be ashamed.

The world today is engulfed by chaos and many issues. It's prevalent in governments, schools, the private sectors, the streets, and even among Christians. There are folks who know what's going on, there are folks who know why it is happening, and there are folks who don't have the intellectual ability or stamina to effect change.

As I scrolled through the entire chapter, I couldn't help but to pay special attention to Joel 2:12–14:

> Therefore also now, says the Lord, turn you even to me with all your heart, and with fasting, and weeping, and with mourning. And rend your heart, and not your garments, and turn to the Lord your God: for He is gracious and merciful, slow to anger, and of great kindness, and repents Him of evil. Who knows if He will return and repent, and leave a blessing behind Him; even a meat offering and a drink offering to the Lord your God?

My assessment of this portion of scripture suggests, then, that God has made Himself available. He's willing to immediately resolve to these heinous activities, but it's now up to you to activate His hands. He is our refuge and strength and a present help in times of trouble. He is merciful and will come to your rescue, and so He's appealing to the church to repent, return, and be restored. In a nutshell He is saying, "I am the way. I am the solution."

In Psalm 24:1, we see that the earth is the Lord's, and the fullness thereof, which means the world and they that dwell therein. Matthew 6:33 says, "But seek ye first the Kingdom of God, and His righteousness; and all these things shall be added to you." Put first things first.

There are so many scriptures in the Bible that suggest that God's intention is to prosper His people. He has a will for His people. But right now, the issue is that too many of His children are following the way that seems right, lusting after the things of the world. In other words, their focus is on the wrong thing. Some people don't know how to keep their eyes or their hands off things that don't belong to them and desperately desire to follow after everything besides righteousness. But you have been risen with Christ, so it's of major significance to eradicate those fleshy behaviors.

So many don't know that there is a difference between right and good. Right is produced by God. The ways of God are always right. However, just because an action is good does not mean it is automatically beneficial.

Read 1 Corinthians 10:5–10:

> But with many of them God was not well pleased: for they were overthrown in the wilderness. Now these things were our examples, to the intent we should not lust after evil things, as they also lusted. Neither be ye idolaters, as were some of them; as it is written, The people sat down to eat and drink, and rose up to play. Neither let us commit fornication, as some of them committed, and fell in one day three and twenty thousand. Neither let us tempt Christ, as some of them also tempted, and were destroyed

of serpents. Neither murmur ye, as some of them also murmured, and were destroyed of the destroyer.

You will see that this type of behavior isn't anything new. Just as the behavior was present in the Corinthian church, it is present today. Same game, different players.

Take a closer look in your Bible, and with a fuller understanding of the contents, you will observe that every spoken word of God is literally a command. Knowing what commands are, you should also know that they are accompanied by consequences. These consequences, however, can be deadly or beneficial, depending on your response to the command.

Steadfastness in Christ happens to be a personal challenge. It is a vow that every believer has made and must maintain. Let me remind you that the Bible says it's okay to make vows, but you must stand by them. In that way you'll know that God blesses faithfulness.

As Joel 2:23 says, "Be glad then, you children of Zion, and rejoice in the Lord your God: for He has given you the former rain moderately, and He will cause to come down for you the rain, the former rain, and the latter rain in the first month." I'm understanding more than enough, which in a nutshell, interprets abundance or overflow, and it's consistency.

This suggests, then, that you shouldn't be stressed out about anything. You shouldn't be complaining and walking around unsatisfied. Deuteronomy 7:15 says, "And the Lord will take away from thee all sickness, and will put none of the evil diseases of Egypt, which thou knowest, upon thee; but will lay them upon all them that hate thee." God will even give your sicknesses and diseases to those who hate you. The equation is simple: obey God and He will bring you an overflow.

So many times as Christians, we are worried about what we don't see. Some believers are more fearful than the people in the world. They worry about what society has to say, about why people don't like them, and about the activities going on in the enemy's camp. They worry about why they are threatening to take their jobs, about how the bills are going to be paid, and about what they're going to eat today or tomorrow. I'm not qualified for the position. They are holding my past against me. Shut up, stop complaining, and see Him for who He is.

Jesus advised us not worry according to Matthew 6:26-24.
Matthew 6:26-34 (KJV)

Behold the fowls of the air: for they sow not, neither do they reap, nor gather into barns; yet your heavenly Father feedeth them. Are ye not much better than they?

Which of you by taking thought can add one cubit unto his stature?

And why take ye thought for raiment? Consider the lilies of the field, how they grow; they toil not, neither do they spin:

And yet I say unto you, That even Solomon in all his glory was not arrayed like one of these.

Wherefore, if God so clothe the grass of the field, which to day is, and to morrow is cast into the oven, shall he not much more clothe you, O ye of little faith?

Therefore take no thought, saying, What shall we eat? or, What shall we drink? or, Wherewithal shall we be clothed?

(For after all these things do the Gentiles seek:) for your heavenly Father knoweth that ye have need of all these things.

But seek ye first the kingdom of God, and his righteousness; and all these things shall be added unto you.

Take therefore no thought for the morrow: for the morrow shall take thought for the things of itself. Sufficient unto the day is the evil thereof.

Jesus also said in John14:6 (KJV), "I am the way." Let me ask you a question. If God be for you, who can be against you? Start prophesying. Tell yourself, "I am the head and not the tail. I am above and not beneath. I am the lender and not the borrower. I'm rich. I'm strong. I'm grateful, and right now, I'm healed. Look what the Lord has done. I'm here to testify of His goodness and not to complain. I'm here to give thanks and praise. I'm blessed forevermore. He's got this."

Oh ye of little faith, You said your Father owns the cattle on a thousand hills. You said He is rich in houses and lands. You said your Father is the King of glory, so start acting like royalty because this king is the Lord strong and mighty, the Lord mighty in battle. Tell yourself there is therefore now no condemnation to those who are in Christ Jesus, who walk not after the flesh but after the Spirit. He told me that He'll supply all my needs. He has thrown my sins and iniquities in the sea of forgetfulness and will remember them no more.

Tell yourself, "I've been risen with Christ, and I'm in pursuit of those things that are above. My mind is situated in heavenly places where He is seated at the right hand of the Father." Don't you know that you are a royal priesthood, a holy nation, and a peculiar people, and who the Son sets free is free indeed. If you are an eagle, stop acting like a pigeon.

Today you have bragging rights. You should be rejoicing in the Lord because who He keeps is well kept. The earth is your inheritance. The wealth of the wicked is definitely laid up for the righteous. What are you fearful of? Fret not yourself because of evildoers. Neither be thou envious against the workers of iniquity because they have their day.

You were not given the spirit of fear but of love and of a sound mind. You have been set free by the grace of God. So this morning position yourself, for the overflow is on the way.

Isiah 54:17 says, "No weapon that is formed against you shall prosper, and every tongue that shall rise against you in judgement, You shall condemn. This is the heritage of the servants of the Lord, and their righteousness is of me, says the Lord." This has nothing to do with you. God will watch over His word to perform it. He will fight your battle and continue to lift up a standard on your behalf when the enemy comes in like a flood.

Verse 25 speaks specifically to your faith, the now faith. This faith has the ability to reach way into your history and disqualify everything the enemy has contaminated and has stolen. It will free your present state from the chains of darkness so that whatever or whoever was devouring your resources, be it the court, the grocery store, business partners, evil friends, sweetheart, drugs, or alcohol, will be defeated, and it will make you restoration worthy.

We're talking about a God who is an expert in the impossibilities. The Bible says that nothing is impossible with God, so know today that when you are down to nothing, God is always up to something. I've stopped by to tell somebody that if you repent and return to God, He will restore you.

Rejoice and be exceedingly glad because your overflow is in sight. The Bible says that eyes have not seen, ears haven't heard, and neither has it entered into the hearts of men what God has in store for you. There's just one condition—humble yourselves, pray, seek His face, and turn from your wicked ways. He will hear from heaven, forgive your sins, and position you for your overflow.

Many today want an overflow, but not many want to follow the requirements, which is to refrain from their conniving ways and deeds, an awful mind set, get right, and go straight. I can tell you, nasty minds are destroying the very fabric of the church. It's good to sit in the house of God and pretend that you have it all together. You know who you are, and you know what you have to do. Nothing changes in life until you do.

I have read in Isaiah 1:18a (KJV), "Come now, and let us reason together says the Lord." Isaiah 1:19 (KJV) goes on to say, "If ye be willing and obedient, you shall eat the good of the land." This morning, the topic speaks of an overflow, but the key to an overflow is obedience. When you are obedient, you'll have a high expectation from God, so I want you to understand that unless you are living a righteous, holy life, He can't bless you. In other words, you will get nothing and you shouldn't be expecting anything either, other than the wages of sin. Isaiah 1:20 (KJV) says, "But if ye refuse and rebel, ye shall be devoured with the sword: for the mouth of the Lord hath spoken it."

I often hear Christians saying, "I'm sowing this seed into this or that one's life, but I'm not expecting anything," So please tell me, what are you expecting? No one sow seeds without the expectation of a harvest.

I've noticed with church folks, especially Pentecostal denominations, that they don't exercise prolonged faith (patience). They don't have the ability to wait, and a whole lot don't know how to satisfy. I want it all, and I want it now. God said it, and I want it. Life is divided into three aspects. First is the promise, followed by the process and then the product.

Numbers 23:19 says, "God is not a man that He should lie, neither is he the son of man that he should repent." If He says it, learn to wait. You want the promise and the product but not the criteria. (Learn to wait.)

Today the overflow is here, and you can walk in it. You can leave here with it, but there are some things you have to put an end to. I'll share a few with you.

- Stop wheeling and dealing with Nebuchadnezzar.
- Purify your thoughts.
- Let go of your neighbor.
- Learn to forgive and let go of the past.
- Fall in love with the truth, and stop getting upset when people are pointing you in the right direction. Stop spreading rumors. God hates the feet that are swift to mischief.
- Humble yourself and apologize to people you've been hurting without a cause.

Ask God to search you, know your heart, test you, know your thoughts, and scope out and dismantle the wicked ways in you. Ask Him to create in you a clean heart and renew a right spirit in you.

Walk away from double-standard living. Turn loose the grip you have on other people's spouses. Stand up for holiness, and stand up for righteousness. Psalm 55:23 says that a bloody and deceitful man shall not live out half his days.

There are too many wearing a form of godliness and who are denying the power. There is too much fashion, shaking, and shouting. False pretenses are wreaking havoc on the house of God. I'm sorry to report to you that the church is in serious trouble. Folks are still speaking in tongues, prophesying, singing, preaching, shouting, all while knowing that the Holy Spirit left them a long time ago.

They know that they've been turned over to a reprobate mind, and like Saul, the spirit of pride is holding them in place, but their purpose was revoked. Everywhere you turn, churches are popping out of the ground like popcorn because people don't want to reconcile, don't want to forgive, and don't want to humble themselves. Not many have Jesus.

Eradicate these spiritual infractions. God says you shall eat plentifully, be satisfied, and praise the name of the Lord your God, who has dealt wondrously with you. And you'll never be ashamed.

And you shall know that He is in the midst of you, and that He is the Lord your God, and no other, and His people shall never be ashamed.

Today, God has spoken. He will send you an overflow.

God bless you. God keep you.

CHAPTER 9

An Expected End

Jeremiah 29:8–14 (KJV)

For thus saith the Lord of hosts, the God of Israel; Let not your prophets and your diviners, that be in the midst of you, deceive you, neither hearken to your dreams which ye cause to be dreamed.

For they prophesy falsely unto you in my name: I have not sent them, saith the Lord.

For thus saith the Lord, That after seventy years be accomplished at Babylon I will visit you, and perform my good word toward you, in causing you to return to this place.

For I know the thoughts that I think toward you, saith the Lord, thoughts of peace, and not of evil, to give you an expected end.

Then shall ye call upon me, and ye shall go and pray unto me, and I will hearken unto you.

And ye shall seek me, and find me, when ye shall search for me with all your heart.

And I will be found of you, saith the Lord:
and I will turn away your captivity, and I will
gather you from all the nations, and from all the
places whither I have driven you, saith the Lord;
and I will bring you again into the place whence
I caused you to be carried away captive.

As you look around in the world today, you can't help but to notice how so many people are wrapped and tangled up in the cares of this world. It's amazing to see how folks live their lives with an aim to please everybody but God.

They will tell you, "I've got to do it the government's way or the way the people like it. It's simply the way that seems right. I may not get the recognition of the hierarchy. This may stop or delay my expectations. I've got to sell out and release my integrity because I don't want to disappoint anyone." Big headline—sorry to tell you, but you are a disappointment already.

Has anyone ever stopped and wondered whether he or she is doing the things that please God? Has anyone ever acknowledged God before executing any of these physical assignments? Had they done that, things would have been very different.

The Bible says in Proverbs 3:6 (KJV) that in all your ways, you should acknowledge God and He will direct your path. This is so He will approve or disapprove your actions or dealings. You must remember that you are not your own. According to 1 Corinthians 6:20, we were bought with a price. In other words, we were paid for, so we should honor the purchaser.

The filthy habits and dirty ways should have been aborted a long time ago. It's useless to sit up and pretend that all is well when people can see the difficult times you are experiencing, see the rough roads you are walking, and see the brick walls you are running into. And so many are allowing the way that seems right to just be right. Every child of God has or is entitled to an expected end.

One may ask, what's an expected end all about?

I am pleased to report to you today that the Bible says in the book of Psalms that God will not withhold any good thing from those that walk uprightly before Him. Numbers 23:19 (KJV) says, "God is not a man, that He should lie; neither the son of man, that he should repent: hath he said, and shall he not do it? Or hath he spoken, and shall he not make it good?"

If all this is so, then tell me what went wrong. Why are so many folks on a collision course? Why do so many people want to be eye servants? Perhaps it's a game.

My questions to you today are: Are you acknowledging Him? Are you following His directions? Are you carrying out your God-given duty in a timely manner?

One may say, "Well, how can you tell? You cannot judge me. I answer only to God." Well, brothers and sisters, misses and misters, I have news for you. The Bible says in Proverbs 1:32–33 (KJV), "For the turning away of the simple shall slay them, and the prosperity of fools shall destroy them. But whoso harkeneth unto me shall dwell safely, and shall be quiet from fear of evil."

In other words, a fruit identifies its tree. Apple trees bears apples, not mangoes.

It is time to get it right in the house of God. So you know, any true Spirit-filled shepherd is qualified to make an assessment of his flock.

Many are anticipating an expected end, only to find that their performance was zero. Their positions were filled and their functions were empty. They lived as they wanted to, doing things to please the flesh, dancing to the music of Nebuchadnezzar, living double-standard lives, being liars and gossipmongers, being homosexuals or lesbians, or being witchcraft workers. Romans 1:27–28 says God gave them over to a reprobate mind. In other words, they continued to be who you were.

These people get involved in mischievous acts, including adultery, while bouncing around, clapping, singing, and even holding positions in the house of God, and try to justify it by saying, "Well, my husband or wife does not know how to treat me."

Psalm 55:19–23 (KJV) says:

> God shall hear, and afflict them, even he that abideth of old. Selah. Because they have no changes, therefore they fear not God. He hath put forth his hands against such as be at peace with him: he hath broken his covenant. The words of his mouth was smoother than butter, but war was in his heart: his words were softer than oil, yet were they drawn swords. Cast thy burden upon the Lord, and he shall sustain thee: he shall never suffer the righteousness to be moved. But thou, O God, shall bring them down

into the pit of destruction: bloody and deceitful men shall not live out half of their days; but I will trust in thee.

And you are wondering why so many people are dying in their youth? An expected end has been revoked.

It does not matter how you feel or what you are thinking. Righteousness still exalts a nation, and sin is still a reproach to any people. (Proverbs 14:34 KJV)

We have to get it right or forget an expected end.

When you understand your duty, you'll know the thoughts of God. When you understand your duty, His thoughts come to mind. And just in case you don't know your duty, according to Ecclesiastes 12:13, "Let us hear the conclusion of the whole matter: Fear God, and keep his commandments: for this is the whole duty of man."

The purpose of humankind is to fear God and keep His commandments. Nothing else—just respect Him and obey Him. When you report in for duty, you can't knock off when you feel like it. You have to persevere and be sincerely committed to hear, "Well done." You're looking forward to an expected end.

First Samuel 15:22b says, "Behold, to obey is better than sacrifice, and to harken than the fat of rams."

Jeremiah 29:8–9 (KJV) says, "For thus saith the Lord of hosts, the God of Israel; Let not your prophets and your diviners, that be in the midst of you, deceive you, neither hearken to your dreams which ye cause to be dreamed. For they prophesy falsely unto you in my name: I have not sent them, saith the Lord."

God wants to give each of us an expected end, and for some strange reason, many don't want it or want to get it their way and in their time. So they go to the false prophets and the diviners who come around. You can tell who they are. They are everywhere, just prophesying a bunch of off-the-wall stories, washing the truth out of their hearts and filling them to the brim with lies and false expectations, causing some of the very elect to be deceived.

God is saying in verse 9 that they are prophesying falsely to us in His name. He says, "I want you to focus and get a grip on what is happening. Stir up the gifts that I've placed in you. I did not send them, but some folks are so caught up with their own agendas that when the truth comes, they can't recognize it, so pride and arrogance finish them off."

There's a perfect illustration of this in Philippians 1:6: "Being confident of this very thing, that he which hath begun a good work in you will perform it until the day Of Jesus Christ." You are a work in progress, and He knows by the outcome provided that He is allowed to finish it. He knows what the end looks like. God is in the end and in the beginning at the same time. It means that you will receive a good ending.

I can assure you today that there is absolutely no one who has started off wrong and ended up being right. Once your life is aligned with the Word of God, the Bible says in 2 Chronicles 7:12, when we call upon Him in prayer, He will listen to us. Second Chronicles 7:14 says, "If my people which are called by my name, shall humble themselves, pray, seek my face and turn from their wicked ways, then I will hear from Heaven, forgive their sins and I'll heal the land." Now you can be assured of an expected end.

One of the easiest things to do is to obey God. From time immemorial, the children of Israel were promised an expected end, and for the life of me, I couldn't tell you why when things are given to some people, they can't appreciate them, accept them, and move on.

Instead, the slave mentality kicks in. Folks feel as though there must be some form of torture, struggle, or excruciating procedure for them to believe the thing is real. No one gives you something for nothing. There's a catch to this. To tell you the truth, unless a price is placed on something, the value is not known or appreciated. But the price has already been paid.

God only wanted to take the children of Israel into the Promised Land from a land of slavery; physical, sexual, and mental abuse; and control, but they refused to accept it. It was too easy.

They complained and asked Moses to let them return to Egypt. Their cry was that they could have lived better lives there. Their claim was that they had everything at their fingertips and Moses brought them out into the wilderness to die. This, among other things, made the way for God to fire all over the age of twenty. They were not entitled to an expected end. They were destroyed and without remedy.

Some people prefer to be slaves and servants. They are comfortable being wrongfully handled. They don't need to be released. It's better to be beaten with whips and scorpions than to progress to an expected end.

It's better to be raped and abused than to walk with God. They don't appreciate the promise. Unfortunately, up to this day, nothing has changed. Folks are still living under that curse.

They are satisfied with mediocrity. They can do without. It doesn't matter if they can have their own way. In John 10:10 (KJV), Jesus says, "The thief cometh not, but for to steal, and to kill, and to destroy: I am come that they might have life, and that they might have it more abundantly."

In Matthew 11:28–30 (KJV), He goes on to say, "Come unto me, all ye that labour and are heavy laden, and I will give you rest. Take my yoke upon you, and learn of me; for I am meek and lowly in heart: and ye shall find rest unto your souls. For my yoke is easy, and my burden is light."

Hear this: You may say, Lord, You have to be joking. All my life I had to struggle to get what I wanted. There is no way this thing could be free. They had every excuse in the world. There were giants in the land. Moses was taking too long on the mountain. They were thirsty and hungry. What was next?

They preferred to toe the line with burnt offerings and sacrifices. Jesus showed up to be the ultimate sacrifice, and they rejected Him.

If you want to experience an expected end, these are the requirements:

- You must serve God with your whole heart.
- You must love your neighbors as yourself.
- You must turn loose all those immoral and derogatory things. You know what they are.
- You must stop holding grudges.

Get tired of the jealousy, hatred, greed, witchcraft working, competition, lying, and nasty habits.

Make an about-face. Let go of the gossiping and the

manipulation, and anchor your souls in the haven of rest and sail the wily seas no more. This is the focus for an expected end.

There are scriptures throughout the Bible where you'll see how so many people had to line up and leave some things and places to receive an expected end, including:

> Now the Lord had said unto Abram, Get thee out of thy country, and from thy kindred, and from thy father's house, unto a land that I will shew thee: And I will make of thee a great nation, and I will bless thee, and make thy name great; and thou shalt be a blessing: And I will bless them that bless thee, and curse him that curseth thee: and in thee shall all families of the earth be blessed. (Genesis 12:1–3 KJV)

> And it came to pass, when Joseph was come unto his brethren, that they stript Joseph out of his coat, his coat of many colours that was on him; And they took him, and cast him into a pit: and the pit was empty, there was no water in it. (Genesis 37:23–24 KJV)

It's a serious thing to dream big among small people. Some folks will try to kill you for what you dream. But how many know that they can't kill the dream?

> And there went a man of the house of Levi, and took to wife a daughter of Levi. And the woman conceived, and bare a son: and when she saw him that he was a goodly child, she hid him

three months. And when she could not longer hide him, she took for him an ark of bulrushes, and daubed it with slime and with pitch, and put the child therein; and she laid it in the flags by the river's brink. (Exodus 2:1–3 KJV)

Jesus had to leave heaven, come to earth, and turn Himself in as a criminal. He was fully condemned, was guilty, was crucified, and was buried so you and I could be liberated to achieve an expected end.

Christ hath redeemed us from the curse of the law, being made a curse for us: for it is written, Cursed is every one that hangeth on a tree. (Galatians 3:3 KJV)

Yet some didn't appreciate it, and some right now still don't care to.

I will say to you that God so loved the world that He gave His only begotten Son that whosoever believes in Him shall not perish but have everlasting life. What are you willing to let go? What are you willing to sacrifice? Who are you willing to help? Are you looking forward to an expected end?

I want to encourage you to revive the Spirit of love, bear one another's burdens, turn loose the malice, and tell your neighbors how long you hated them for nothing. Tell them how you used to show up to church to compete and to feel good. Tell them what a pretender you are. Tell your friends how much you secretly despise them and tried to keep them down. Tell them that every time you tried, God has lifted them and opened new doors for them. Tell them how sin and wickedness have you, and you can't see the city for the smoke. Tell them how sowing seeds of discord is killing you. Let them know how you tried every wicked trick in the book and they all failed. Now you want to do it the right way. You want to see Jesus for who He is. You want an expected end like them, and you're looking forward to it.

Ask them to please forgive you because your anticipation for the end is now great. You want what God has for you. My Bible tells me that when the enemy comes in like a flood, the Spirit of the Lord will lift up a standard against Him. Show up for duty, do what you were called to do, and you will hear "Well done." You will have an expected end.

ABOUT THE AUTHOR

In the year 2003, the author answered the call to ministry and developed a passion and a love for Bible studies and teaching that has never stopped since. As time went by, this gift intensified tremendously, and he found himself in his comfort zone. Of all his other accomplishments, he found that his passion truly was teaching, but not in the school system.

To him, Bible studies should happen anytime and anywhere—first thing in the morning and last thing at night, at work, home, or wherever he goes. When he's participating in Bible discussions, he'll be the first to begin. Once the Spirit of revelation takes over and he's done, he'll say, "You should have recorded that because I don't remember a thing."

Wellington also walks in the gifts of wisdom and prophecy. He has very little or nothing to say, but once his mouth opens, he brings much clarity to anything or scripture, as the case may be. Wellington never believed that the sky was the limit as so many have claimed. He has always referred to his God as the limit, and with this understanding, he never believed anything was impossible. Wellington's love and dedication to his family, God, and God's people keeps him focused. He is determined that nothing will separate him from the love of God.

CPSIA information can be obtained
at www.ICGtesting.com
Printed in the USA
BVHW031057310720
585141BV00005B/50